WORLD OF LANGUAGE

SILVER BURDETT & GINN

Nancy Nickell Ragno   Marian Davies Toth   Betty G. Gray

Contributing Author — Primary   Elfrieda Hiebert
Contributing Author — Vocabulary   Richard E. Hodges
Contributing Author — Poetry   Myra Cohn Livingston

Consulting Author — Thinking Skills   David N. Perkins

SILVER BURDETT & GINN
MORRISTOWN, NJ   NEEDHAM, MA
Atlanta, GA   Cincinnati, OH   Dallas, TX   Menlo Park, CA   Deerfield, IL

Acknowledgments

Cover: Howard Berelson

Contributing writers: Jane Allen, Sandra Breuer, Judy Brim, Marcia Miller

Contributing artists: Angela Adams, Cynthia Armine, Bill Bell, Doron Ben-Ami, Lori Bernero, Tom Bobrowski, Kristine Bollinger, Roberta Collier, Gwen Connolly, Floyd Cooper, Rick Cooley, Carolyn Croll, Margaret Cusack, John Cymerman, Frank Daniel, Susan David, Helen Davie, Don Dyen, Len Ebert, Marlene Eckman, Tom Garcia, Bruce Lemerise, Susan Lexa, Richard Loehle, Kathleen McCord, Joseph Mirallis, Kathy Mitchell, Cyd Moore, Karen Nelson, John Nez, Tom Noonan, Loughran O'Connor, Lisa O'Hanlon, Taylor Oughton, Karen Pellaton, Lisa Pomerantz, Marcy Ramsey, Eileen Rosen, Sally Shaedler, Bob Shein, Samantha Smith, Sandra Speidel, Wayne Anthony Still, Susan Swan, Deborah Troyer, Kyuso Tsugami, John Wallner, Paul Wenzel, Jane Yamada, Lane Yerkes

Picture credits: All photographs by Silver Burdett & Ginn (SB&G) unless otherwise noted **Introduction:** 3: *b.l.* Dan DeWilde for SB&G. **Unit 1:** 21: Lawrence Migdale for SB&G. 31: All by IMAGERY for SB&G. 35: All by IMAGERY for SB&G. 38: Dan DeWilde for SB&G. 41: Dan DeWilde for SB&G. 42: Dan DeWilde for SB&G. 43: *t. Jamaica's Find* by Juanita Havill. Text copyright © 1986 by Anne Sibley O'Brien. Reprinted by permission of Houghton Mifflin Company. **Unit 2:** 54: Steven C. Kaufman/Peter Arnold, Inc. 73: Chris Harvey/TSW-Click/Chicago, Ltd. 78: Dan DeWilde for SB&G. 81: Dan DeWilde for SB&G. 82: Brian Parker/Tom Stack & Associates. 83: *t. Q Is for Duck* by Mary Elting and Michael Folsom. Text copyright © 1980 by Mary Elting and Michael Folsom. Illustrations copyright © 1980 by Jack Kent. Reprinted by permission of Clarion Books/Ticknor & Fields, a Houghton Mifflin Company. **Unit 3:** 116: Dan DeWilde for SB&G. 119: Dan DeWilde for SB&G. 120: Marcello Bertiretti/Photo Researchers, Inc. 121: *t. The Star Maiden* by Barbara Juster Esbensen. Text © 1988 by Barbara Juster Esbensen. Cover illustration © 1988 by Helen K. Davie. Used by permission of Little, Brown and Company. 121: *b.* Dan DeWilde for SB&G. **Unit 4:** 154: Dan DeWilde for SB&G. 157: Dan DeWilde for SB&G. 159: *t. The Rooster Crows* by Maud and Miska Petersham. Copyright 1945 by Macmillan Publishing Company, renewed 1973 by Miska F. Petersham. Reproduced with permission of Macmillan Publishing Company. **Unit 5:** 168: *Cloudy with a Chance of Meatballs* by Judi Barrett. Illustrations copyright © 1978 by Ron Barrett. Reprinted by permission of Atheneum Publishers, an imprint of Macmillan Publishing Company. *Frog and Toad Together* by Arnold Lobel. Copyright © 1971, 1972 by Arnold Lobel. Published by Harper & Row, Publishers, Inc. *Just Us Women* by Jeannette Caines, illustrated by Pat Cummings. Text copyright © 1982 by Jeannette Franklin Caines. Illustrations copyright © 1982 by Pat Cummings. Published by Harper & Row, Publishers, Inc. *Knots on a Counting Rope* by Bill Martin Jr. and John Archambault. Illustrated by Ted Rand. Used courtesy of Henry Holt & Company. 193: Dan DeWilde for SB&G. 194: Dan DeWilde for SB&G. 197: Dan DeWilde for SB&G. 199: *t. Three Days on a River in a Red Canoe* by Vera B. Williams. Copyright © 1981 by Vera B. Williams. Used by permission of Greenwillow Books (A division of William Morrow & Company, Inc.). **Unit 6:** 231: Quilt pieced by Sherri Hieber-Day, quilted by Wealtha Drake. 234: Dan DeWilde for SB&G. 237: Dan DeWilde for SB&G. 239: *t. The Quilt Story* by Tony Johnston. Illustration © 1985 by Tomie dePaola. Used by permission of G.P. Putnam's Sons. **Unit 7:** 262: *t.* Kim Taylor/Bruce Coleman; *b.* J.P. Myers/Vireo/H. Armstrong Roberts. 263: *t.* James P. Rowan/TSW-Click/Chicago, Ltd.; *b.* Robert C. Simpson/Tom Stack & Associates. 264: *l.* © Bill Bachman/Photo Researchers, Inc. 265: *t.* Shostal Associates; *m.* © 1990 Ed Bock/The Stock Market. 270: Dan DeWilde for SB&G. 273: Dan DeWilde for SB&G. 274: © 1990 Lee L.Waldman/The Stock Market. 275: *t. The Cloud Book* by Tomie dePaola. Copyright © 1975 by Tomie dePaola. Reprinted by permission of Holiday House. **Unit 8:** 278: Courtesy Jim Gary. 293–298: All courtesy Jim Gary. 300: *l.* Will McIntyre/Photo Researchers, Inc. 301: *Making Sense of Money* by Vicki Cobb. Copyright © 1971 by Vicki Cobb. Used by permission of Parents Magazine Press. 303: *l. Bea and Mr. Jones* by Amy Schwartz. Copyright © 1982 by Amy Schwartz. Reproduced with permission of Bradbury Press, an affiliate of Macmillan, Inc.; *m. Fire! Fire!* by Gail Gibbons. Jacket art copyright © 1984 by Gail Gibbons. Reprinted by permission of Harper & Row, Publishers, Inc. (Thomas Y. Crowell); *r. The Berenstain Bears on the Job* by Stanley and Janie Berenstain. Copyright © by Random House, Inc. 305: *m.t.* Joe Viesti for SB&G; *m.b.* Kjell B. Sandved/Photo Researchers, Inc. 308: Courtesy Jim Gary. 310: Dan DeWilde for SB&G. 312: Dan DeWilde for SB&G. 313: Dan DeWilde for SB&G. 315: *t. Martin's Hats* by Joan W. Blos. Copyright © 1984 by Joan W. Blos. Illustrations copyright © 1984 by Marc Simont. Used by permission of Morrow Junior Books (A division of William Morrow & Company, Inc.); *m.* and *b.* Dan DeWilde for SB&G.

Acknowledgments continued on page 344

· CONTENTS ·

INTRODUCTORY UNIT

UNIT 1

USING LANGUAGE TO PERSUADE

══════════════════ **PART ONE** ══════════════════

LANGUAGE AWARENESS ◆ SENTENCES

══════════════════ **PART TWO** ══════════════════

A REASON FOR WRITING ◆ PERSUADING

UNIT 2

USING LANGUAGE TO CLASSIFY

UNIT 3

USING LANGUAGE TO IMAGINE

═══════════════════ PART ONE ═══════════════════

LANGUAGE AWARENESS ♦ VERBS

═══════════════════ PART TWO ═══════════════════

A REASON FOR WRITING ♦ IMAGINING

UNIT 4

USING LANGUAGE TO CREATE

UNIT 5

USING LANGUAGE TO INFORM

──────────── PART ONE ────────────

LANGUAGE AWARENESS ♦ NOUNS and PRONOUNS

──────────── PART TWO ────────────

A REASON FOR WRITING ♦ INFORMING

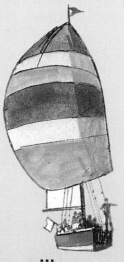

UNIT 6

USING LANGUAGE TO NARRATE

═══════════════════ PART ONE ═══════════════════

LANGUAGE AWARENESS ◆ VERBS

═══════════════════ PART TWO ═══════════════════

A REASON FOR WRITING ◆ NARRATING

UNIT 7

USING LANGUAGE TO DESCRIBE

————————————————— PART ONE —————————————————

LANGUAGE AWARENESS ♦ ADVERBS

————————————————— PART TWO —————————————————

A REASON FOR WRITING ♦ DESCRIBING

UNIT 8

USING LANGUAGE TO RESEARCH

━━━━━━━━━━━━━━━ PART ONE ━━━━━━━━━━━━━━━

LANGUAGE AWARENESS ♦ SENTENCES

━━━━━━━━━━━━━━━ PART TWO ━━━━━━━━━━━━━━━

A REASON FOR WRITING ♦ RESEARCHING

WRITER'S REFERENCE BOOK

AWARD
◆ LITERATURE ◆
WINNING

I Know a Lady
by Charlotte Zolotow
pictures by James Stevenson

The Paper Crane
by Molly Bang

Stringbean's Trip to the Shining Sea
by Vera B. Williams
and Jennifer Williams

Owl Moon
by Jane Yolen
illustrated by John Schoenherr

The Josefina Story Quilt
by Eleanor Coerr
pictures by Bruce Degan

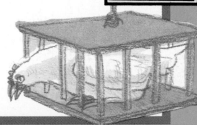

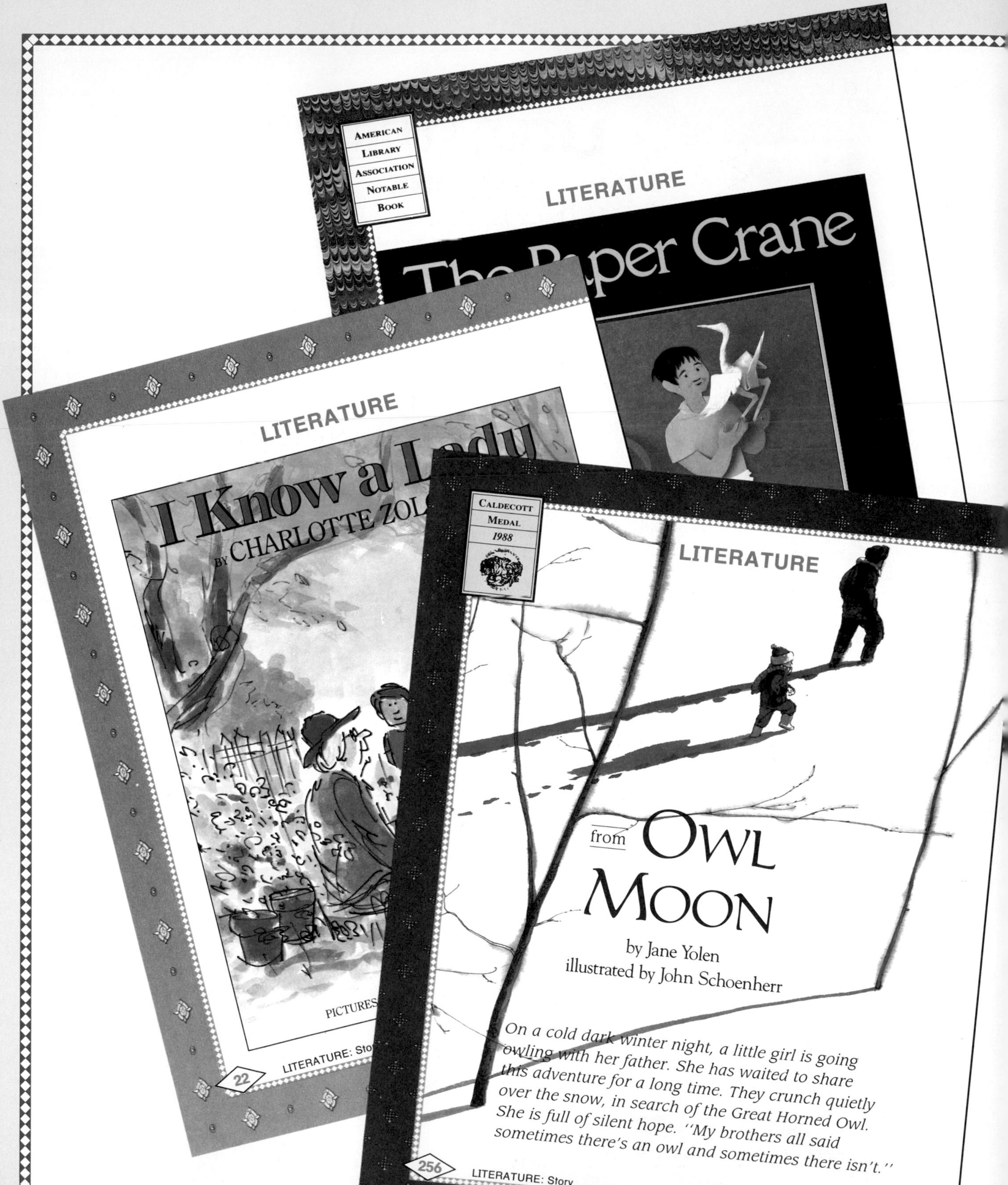

AMERICAN LIBRARY ASSOCIATION NOTABLE BOOK

LITERATURE

The Paper Crane

LITERATURE

I Know a Lady

BY CHARLOTTE ZOL

PICTURES

LITERATURE: Sto

22

CALDECOTT MEDAL 1988

LITERATURE

from OWL MOON

by Jane Yolen

illustrated by John Schoenherr

On a cold dark winter night, a little girl is going owling with her father. She has waited to share this adventure for a long time. They crunch quietly over the snow, in search of the Great Horned Owl. She is full of silent hope. ''My brothers all said sometimes there's an owl and sometimes there isn't.''

256

LITERATURE: Story

Introductory Unit

Literature in Your World

Literature is a key. It unlocks your imagination. It opens your mind to a world of ideas. With literature you can enter any time or any place. You can meet people you would never really meet. You can have great adventures! Literature is a key to your world and the wonderful world of language.

Writing in Your World

Writing and reading work together. They are partners, a team. Writing is read by readers. Sometimes you write for others, and sometimes for yourself. Writing helps you share your ideas. Writing helps you grow.

Writing is thinking. When you write, you capture your ideas — and you let your imagination run free.

Writing helps you find out about your world. Writing can help you change it! Writing is powerful. It is a powerful tool for you in your wonderful world of language.

What Is a Writer?

A writer is anyone who writes. Do you write your name? Do you write sentences? Do you write words on your pictures? Then you are already a writer.

Writing for Yourself ♦ Sometimes you show your writing to someone. Other times you may write just for yourself. You can write for yourself in a journal.

Journal Writing

A journal can be in a notebook. It can be some pages pinned together. What can you write in your journal?

♦ You can draw and label pictures.
♦ You can tell what happens each day.
♦ You can practice your math.

In your journal you can write anything you want to.

Introducing the Writing Process

Sometimes you want to write something to share with others. You want to make it really good. The writing process can help you.

The writing process is a helpful plan for writing. First you get ideas to write about. Then you write. Next you make changes to make it better. Finally you share your writing.

THINK, READ, SPEAK, LISTEN, WRITE

Many lessons will help you get ready to write.

THINKING

- **Thinking skill** lessons teach one special way to think. You can use them when you read and write.

- **Literature** lessons show how grown-up authors write. You can get ideas for your own writing.

LISTENING   SPEAKING

- **Speaking and listening** lessons help you get ready to write.

- **Writing** lessons teach skills you can use in the writing process.

WRITING

READING

Using the Writing Process

Write a Description

Read the next four pages. They tell about the five steps of the writing process. The activities will help you try each step.

1 Prewriting ♦ Getting ready to write

Before you write, you need to think of some ideas. You need to have ideas to write about.

How can you get ideas to write about? There are lots of ways. You can look at something. You can draw it. You can talk with a partner about it.

PREWRITING IDEA

Using Your Senses

Look around your classroom. What is the prettiest thing you see?

Observe Maybe you chose a flower on your teacher's desk. Look at it carefully. Does it have a smell? How does it feel? Draw it. Write words about it on your picture.

2 Writing ♦ Putting your ideas on paper

Now you will write sentences to describe the thing you chose.

What if you make a mistake? Don't worry. Just start writing. You can fix any mistakes later.

WRITING IDEA

Naming Something

Look at the picture you drew. Then start to write about it.

How can you begin? You may name what you chose that is pretty. You could write <u>The pink flower is pretty</u>.

Then write about what you chose. Tell how it looks. Maybe you can also tell how it feels or smells.

3 Revising ♦ Making changes to improve your writing.

When you finish writing, read what you wrote. Do you like it? Do you wish you could add a word? Do you want to take a word out?

Writers often make changes to make their writing better. You can, too.

REVISING IDEA

Read to Yourself and to a Partner

First read what you wrote to yourself. Then read it aloud to a partner.

Do you think you left out any important words? Write them above the line. Cross out words you don't want. Your partner can help you decide what to change.

4 Proofreading ♦ Looking for and fixing errors

Check your writing to be sure it is correct. Then make a neat copy.

5 Publishing ♦ Sharing your writing with others

You can share your writing in many ways. You can read it aloud. You can let others read it.

Illustration by James Stevenson

UNIT ONE

USING LANGUAGE TO
PERSUADE

=== PART ONE ===

Unit Theme   *Special Friends*

Language Awareness   Sentences

=== PART TWO ===

Literature   *I Know a Lady* by Charlotte Zolotow

A Reason for Writing   Persuading

Writing
IN YOUR JOURNAL

WRITER'S WARM-UP ◆ Friends are very important people. You may have friends at home, in your class, or in your neighborhood. Who is one of your friends? Write about your friend in your journal. Tell why he or she is special to you.

1

Sentences

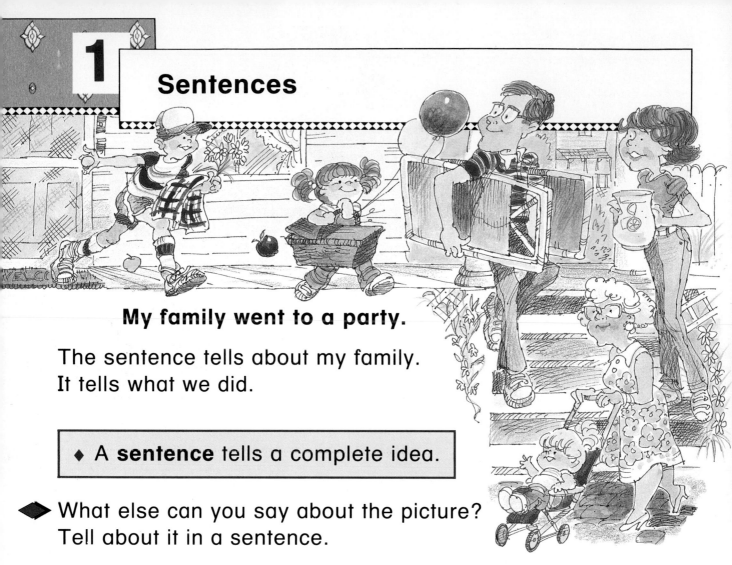

My family went to a party.

The sentence tells about my family.
It tells what we did.

♦ A **sentence** tells a complete idea.

◆ What else can you say about the picture?
Tell about it in a sentence.

◆ Which picture does each sentence tell about?
Match each sentence with a picture.

1. Peggy held the basket.　　**a.**

2. Dad took some chairs.　　**b.**

3. Bob closed the door.　　**c.**

The neighbors
The neighbors have fun.

Some groups of words are not sentences.
The neighbors is not a sentence.
It does not tell what the neighbors do.
The neighbors have fun. is a sentence.

◆ Write the sentence from each pair.

4. a. Our family arrives.　　**b.** Our family

5. a. The sun　　　　　　　**b.** The sun comes out.

6. a. My friends　　　　　　**b.** My friends play.

7. a. The girl jumps high.　　**b.** The girl

8. a. The food is ready.　　　**b.** The delicious food

Apply　　What would you bring to a party?
Tell about it. Remember to use sentences.

Statements

The girl makes a card.

- ◆ Begin a sentence with a **capital letter.**
- ◆ End a **telling sentence,** or **statement,** with a **period** $\boxed{\cdot}$.

Write the correct statement from each pair.

1. **a.** Sue cuts the paper.   **b.** sue cuts the paper

2. **a.** the flower is pretty   **b.** The flower is pretty.

3. **a.** it is ready now   **b.** It is ready now.

4. **a.** They walk down.   **b.** they walk down

5. **a.** A friend lives here.   **b.** a friend lives here

6. **a.** they surprise him   **b.** They surprise him.

◆ Write each statement correctly.

7. they help a friend today

8. he is happy to see them

◆ **9–10.** Write two statements about the picture.
Think about what is happening here.
The words in the box will help you.

broom	floor	helps	sweeps
card	friend	man	plant
clean	girl	mother	water

Apply Do you ever help someone?
Write a statement about what you do.

3 Questions

When does the pet show begin?

- Begin a sentence with a capital letter.
- End an **asking sentence,** or **question,** with a **question mark** $\boxed{?}$.

◆ Write the correct question from each pair.

1. **a.** Is that your cat?   **b.** is that your cat

2. **a.** what is its name   **b.** What is its name?

3. **a.** did you see my birds   **b.** Did you see my birds?

4. **a.** Can they both sing?   **b.** can they both sing

5. **a.** which dog does tricks   **b.** Which dog does tricks?

6. **a.** How can you tell?   **b.** how can you tell

Write the question from each pair.

7. **a.** How many spots are on that dog?
   b. You cannot count all the spots.

8. **a.** The birds sing all day.
   b. What songs can the birds sing?

9. **a.** Kim did not bring her fish.
   b. Which pet did Ray bring?

10. **a.** Does Dara have a rabbit?
    b. There are two dogs here.

11. **a.** Jean counts the ribbons.
    b. Will every pet get a prize?

12. **a.** When is our next pet show?
    b. We can plan it together.

Apply Do you know someone who has a pet?
What would you like to know about that pet?
Write a question that you might ask the owner.

4 Parts of a Sentence

The boy **takes pictures.**

The boy names who the sentence is about.

takes pictures. tells what the boy does.

> ◆ A sentence has two parts. It has a
> **naming part** and a **telling part**.

◆ Match the sentence parts.
Then say each complete sentence.

1. The baby   **a.** shines today.

2. The sun   **b.** sit on the bench.

3. Lucy   **c.** holds a rattle.

4. Her parents   **d.** goes down the slide.

◆ Copy each sentence.
Draw one line under the naming part.
Draw two lines under the telling part.

5. Aaron shows his pictures.

6. The baby sits in a stroller.

7. Nobody uses the swings.

8. Rosa looks happy.

9. The sun is bright.

10. Tim climbs up.

Apply What part is missing from each sentence?
Think of a naming part or a telling part.
Then write the complete sentences.

11. My friend ___.

12. ___ come to the park.

5 Word Order in Sentences

by sat We campfire. the
We sat by the campfire.

The first group of words is not a sentence.
It is not in an order that makes sense.
We sat by the campfire. is a sentence.

◆ Write the groups of words that are sentences.

1. **a.** sang They songs. many
   b. They sang many songs.

2. **a.** Did you know that one?
   b. one? know Did that you

3. **a.** He told me about camp.
   b. about told camp. He me

4. **a.** new We friends. met
   b. We met new friends.

Write the words in sentence order.

5. games. many I play

6. He ball. the hits

7. the lake. We in swim

8. go fishing. Some boys

9. fish? that see Did you

10. catches net. Paul in it the

 Read the story.
Put each group of words in sentence order.

We helped tent his Ronnie with.
It easy was not.
The tent over almost fell.
Then laughed everyone.
Next time pull tight we will the ropes.

Some stars look very big.
Some stars look very large.

The words **big** and **large** are synonyms.
They mean almost the same thing.

> ◆ **Synonyms** are words that have almost the same meaning.

◆ Write each sentence below.
Use these words as synonyms for the words in dark type.

begins   shine   almost   sees   tired   go

1. Joe **watches** the stars **glow.**

2. He **starts** to feel **sleepy.**

3. It is **nearly** time to **leave.**

Write these words in Joe's story.
Use a synonym for each word in ( ).

| woods | glad | like | build |
| night | dark | put |

Last (evening) __a__ the sky was

very (black) __b__ . My brother (placed) __c__

his telescope near the (forest) __d__ . I was

(happy) __e__ to see the stars.

Today I will (make) __f__ a model

with my brother. I really (enjoy) __g__

having fun with him.

 Write a synonym for each word below.

say   little   street   nice

Now share your work with a friend.
Did you write the same synonyms?

Combining Parts of Sentences

You can put together, or **combine**, two sentences with the same naming part. Use **and** to combine the telling parts.

> **A. The children** clapped.
> **B. The children** cheered.
> **A + B. The children** clapped cheered.

You can also use **and** to put together two sentences with the same telling part. What naming parts are combined below?

> **C.** Pete **joined the team.**
> **D.** Amanda **joined the team.**
> **C + D.** Pete and Amanda **joined the team.**

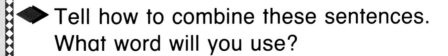 Tell how to combine these sentences. What word will you use?

1. **Mary** raced. **Tanya** raced.

2. Their friends **watched**. Their friends **waved**.

Working Together

Your group can combine parts of sentences using the word **and**.

◆ Choose any two sentences below. Combine the words in dark type using the word **and**. Now try two more sentences. How many can you write?

We **read stories**.   We **play games**.
We **sing songs**.   We **use computers**.
We **write letters**.   We **paint pictures**.

◆ Use **and** to combine the sentence parts in dark type. Then have your group choose new naming parts, such as **My friends** or **Our group**. Write the sentences.

1. **Lee** skated fast. **Jason** skated fast.

2. **Ben** can swim. **Ramona** can swim.

3. **Ruth** cooked. **Willy** cooked.

4. **Erin** read a book. **Luis** read a book.

5. **Carl** will help. **Eva** will help.

TWO YOUNG GIRLS AT THE PIANO
painting by Pierre Auguste Renoir
The Metropolitan Museum of Art,
Robert Lehman Collection, 1975.

UNIT ONE

USING LANGUAGE
TO
PERSUADE

=== PART TWO ===

Literature *I Know a Lady* by Charlotte Zolotow
A Reason for Writing Persuading

CREATIVE
Writing

FINE ARTS ◆ The girls in this picture like to sing together. What do you and your best friend like to do together? Write a note to your friend. Tell about something you can do to have fun.

CRITICAL THINKING ♦
A Strategy for Persuading

A Conclusion Sentence

Have you ever met someone new? Will that person be a good friend? How can you decide? You can notice how the person acts. Then you can draw a conclusion. You can decide what you think about that person.

◆ Look at these pictures. Notice what Dan is doing for Amy. Tell what Amy might decide about Dan. What might her conclusion be?

◆ Look at this picture. Notice what the girl is doing. What is your conclusion about her? Finish the sentence.

I think the girl is___.

CRITICAL THINKING: Drawing Conclusions

◆ Read this story. Then look at the picture.
Decide what you think about Carlos.
Finish the sentence below the picture.

      Saturday is Mom's birthday. Carlos
knows she likes flowers. Carlos has
found some pretty flowers. He gives
them to Mom.

I think Carlos is ____ .

    Next you will read *I Know a Lady*. Look at
the story pictures. What is the lady doing?
What kind of person do you think she is?

Apply

◆ How did you decide what you thought
about Carlos?

◆ Do you ever draw a conclusion about
someone? When?

I Know a Lady

BY CHARLOTTE ZOLOTOW

PICTURES BY JAMES STEVENSON

On our block there is a lady who lives alone.

She works in her garden and gives us
daffodils in the spring, zinnias in the summer,
chrysanthemums in the fall,
and red holly berries when the snow falls.

LITERATURE: Story

She waves to us mornings
on our way to school and smiles
when we pass her house coming home.

She invites us in to warm up
at her fire at Halloween
and gives us candy apples
she's made herself.

Sometimes we see her walking alone
along the path in the woods behind the houses.
She smiles at me and knows my name is Sally.
She pats my dog and knows her name is Matilda.
She feeds the birds and puts cream out
for the old cat who lives across the meadow.

LITERATURE: Story

I wonder what she was like
when she was a little girl.
I wonder if some old lady she knew
had a garden and cooked and smiled
and patted dogs and fed the cats
and knew her name.

If I was an old lady
and she was a little girl
I would love her a lot
the way I do now.

Library Link ◆ *If you liked reading this story by Charlotte Zolotow, look for her other books about friendship,* The White Marble *and* The Summer Night.

 Reader's Response

Do you think the lady in this story is a special person? Tell why.

I Know a Lady

 ## Responding to Literature

1. Could someone your age do the things the lady did for others? Why or why not?

2. With a partner, take turns pretending to be the lady and a child. How did you feel being the lady and being the child?

3. What special thing could you do for someone? Who would you do it for?

 ## Writing to Learn

Think and Create ♦ Draw a medal to give as a thank-you for doing something special.

I think Grandpa is special because he reads funny stories to me.

Conclusion Sentence

Write ♦ Who should get your medal? Write the things your person has done. Then write a sentence that says, I think ___ is special because ___ .

When you talk with other people, you have a **discussion**. A discussion lets you share ideas. You can make plans. You can discuss a problem. A discussion helps you learn from others.

◆ Think about being a good friend.
Write an idea you would like to discuss.

◆ Have a class discussion.
Talk about being a friend.
Follow the rules for a good discussion.

Apply Think about your class discussion.
Which rule was hardest to follow?
Tell your ideas. Did others agree with you?

Giving Directions

These rules can help you give directions.

How to Give Directions

1. Speak clearly.
2. Tell what to do, one step at a time.
3. Tell the steps in the correct order.
4. Begin each step with words like **first**, **next**, **then**, and **last**.

◆ Tell how to carve a pumpkin.
Remember to use words like **first**, **next**, **then**, and **last**.

1.

2.

3.

4.

Apply   Give directions to a friend.
Tell how to ride a bike.
Remember to give the steps in order.

Following Directions

You follow directions when you do your schoolwork. You also follow directions when you play games and use recipes. Why is it important to follow directions?

How to Follow Directions

1. Listen carefully to all of the directions.
2. Follow the directions in the correct order.
3. Do not forget any steps.
4. Ask questions if you need help.

Sam wanted to make orange ice pops. Mrs. Hart told him these directions.

1. Pour orange juice into paper cups.
2. Put the cups into the freezer.
3. After two hours put a popstick into each cup. The juice should be almost frozen.
4. Put the cups back into the freezer for three hours.

Sam looked in the freezer the next day. Look at the picture to see what Sam saw.

◆ Read the steps to make orange ice pops. Write the number of the step Sam forgot.

Work with a friend. You read the directions. Have your friend follow them. Your friend will need crayons, a pencil, scissors, glue, and four pieces of colored paper.

1. Draw a design on a piece of paper with crayons.

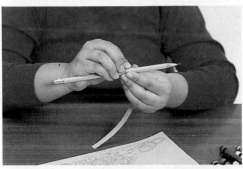

2. Cut long strips from the other pieces of paper.

3. Curl the strips around a pencil.

4. Put glue on the design wherever you would like a paper curl.

5. Press the curls on the glue to make them stick.

Share your picture with the class.

Apply Take turns with a partner.
Give your partner directions to draw a flower.
Have your partner follow the directions.

1. Dial the number carefully.

555-4321

2. Say hello.
Give your name.

Hello, this is Ed Moss.

3. Be polite.

May I please speak to Mr. Gomez?

4. Tell why you are calling.

Mr. Gomez, this is Ed Moss. Could I please visit your puppy?

◆ Work with a partner. Take turns pretending to make these telephone calls.

1. Call a friend. Invite the friend to your school play. Convince your friend to go.

2. Call a pet store.
Find out what toys they sell for puppies.

Apply Pretend there is an emergency.
Tell how you would use the telephone to get help.

Taking a Message

Tim called Carlos to ask him for help.
Carlos was not at home. Read what happened.

Ana: Hello.

Tim: Hello. This is Tim. May I speak to Carlos?

Ana: Hi, Tim. This is Ana. Carlos is out.
May I help you?

Tim: Please give Carlos a message. I would
like him to help me deliver newspapers.
Have him call me at 555-6512. Thank you.

Ana: I'll give Carlos the message. Good-bye.

◆ Write the message Ana should take.
Use a form like this one.

To _____
Who called? _____ Caller's Number _____
Message _____
_____
The message is from _____

◆ Practice making calls and taking messages
with a partner.
Did you write each part of the message?

- ◆ Who the message is for
- ◆ Who called
- ◆ Caller's number
- ◆ Message
- ◆ Who took the message

Writing a Poster Message

You have read the story *I Know a Lady.* The little girl in the story knew a special lady. You found out why she liked the lady. The girl told about the friendly things the lady did. Did she persuade you to like the lady, too?

Now you will write about an older person you like. You will make a poster. On it, you will draw the person. Then you will write why the person is special. Your classmates will look at your poster. Your writing can persuade them that this person is special.

1 Prewriting

Prewriting is getting ready to write. First pick your topic. Then gather ideas.

My Friends
Mrs. Wong
Aunt Rosa
Grandpa

Choose Your Topic ◆ Think of older people who are your friends. You might think of your grandfather. You might pick an aunt or a neighbor. List three older people you like. Then circle one name. This special person will be your topic.

Choose Your Plan ◆ Here are two ways
to get ideas. Try the one you like better.

PREWRITING IDEAS

Plan One ◆ A Picture Chart

Make a picture chart.
Draw little pictures. Show
many nice things about
your person. Write labels
on the pictures.

Plan Two ◆ A Conclusion Sentence

A conclusion is what you think about
something or someone. Think of your person.
Think what is special about him or her. Then
write a conclusion sentence about your person.
Your sentence should begin like this:

I think ___ is special because ___ .

I think Grandpa is special
because he likes to be
with me.

2 Writing

Writing is putting your ideas on paper.

Now you can make your poster. Draw a big picture of your person. Write the person's name at the top.

Save the sentence you wrote for Plan Two. If you did not do Plan Two, write a sentence. Write it on a separate paper. Tell why you think your person is special. Later you can add your sentence to your poster.

3 Revising

Revising is changing your writing to make it better.

Rosa wrote this sentence for her poster. Then she revised it. She added a word. She changed a word.

grandpa is
special bekuz ∧^he^
likes to ~~be~~ ^play ball^ with me.

REVISING IDEA

Read your sentence to yourself. Then ask a partner to listen. Talk about ways you might revise your sentence.

♦ Do you think you'd like my person, too?

♦ Should I add or change any words?

Grammar Check ♦ Does my sentence tell a complete idea?

Now revise your sentence. Show the changes you want to make.

4 Proofreading

Proofreading is looking for and fixing mistakes.

Proofread your poster sentence. These questions may help you.

♦ Did I spell each word correctly?

♦ Did I use capital letters correctly?

♦ Did I use the correct mark at the end of the sentence?

<table>
<tr><td>

PROOFREADING MARKS

◯ check spelling

≡ capital letter

</td></tr>
</table>

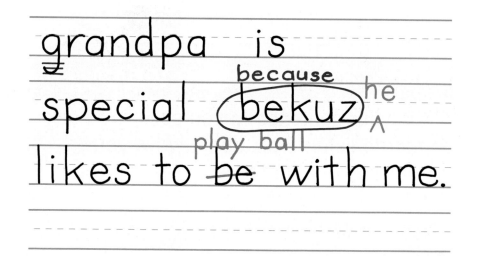

grandpa is special bekuz *because* he *play ball* likes to be with me.

Now your sentence is correct. Copy it neatly at the bottom of your poster.

5 Publishing

Publishing is sharing your writing with others. Here are two ways to share your poster.

PUBLISHING IDEAS

Share Aloud

Stand up and show your poster to your classmates. Then read your sentence aloud. Ask your listeners to tell why your person is special. Each person might tell one thing.

Share in Writing

With your classmates, make a display. Put up your posters on a bulletin board. At the top, put this sentence starter.

Older friends are nice because—

Read and enjoy the posters. Take turns writing an ending to the sentence starter.

Writing for Health and Safety

Friends help each other. Friends look out for each other's safety. You can use writing to show your friends how to be safe. You can persuade them to follow a bicycle safety rule.

Writing to Learn

Think and Decide ♦ What makes a bicycle safe? What rules do you need to obey when you ride a bicycle? Think about it. Then choose one bicycle safety rule. Think about why it is important.

Write ♦ Write a conclusion sentence to tell what you think about following your safety rule.

Writing in Your Journal

In this unit you have read about friends doing things together. Did you discover something new that you might do with a special friend? Write one way to have fun with your friend.

I think _____.

Conclusion Sentence

BOOKS TO ENJOY

◆ Read More About It

We Are Best Friends *by Aliki*
How can best friends stay
friends when one moves away?
Read how two best friends
solve this problem.

Jamaica's Find
by Juanita Havill
A little girl finds a lost toy dog in
the park. Then she finds something
better — a new friend.

◆ Book Report Idea   Mask

Choose a character from a book
you like. Let that character help
you tell about the book. Make a
mask of the character. Use a
paper bag or cardboard. Have
someone cut eye holes for you.
Wear your mask or hold it up as
you tell the class about your book.

Sentences

A. Write the sentence in each pair.

1. **a.** The dog ate dinner.
   b. The dog

2. **a.** A smelly skunk
   b. Max saw a skunk.

3. **a.** Leaped up
   b. A frog leaped up.

4. **a.** Six mice ran home.
   b. Six mice in the field

B. Write each statement correctly.

5. many rabbits hop
6. seals swim fast

7. some dogs bark loudly
8. squirrels eat nuts

C. Write the question from each pair.

9. **a.** Did you go to the zoo?
   b. We went to the zoo.

10. **a.** I got back at noon.
    b. When did you get back?

11. **a.** Zebras have stripes.
    b. Do you like zebras?

12. **a.** Will you go again?
    b. I will go with Sara.

D. Write each question correctly.

13. do ducks quack

14. are ponies small

15. is that a giraffe

16. what do you see

E. Write each sentence. Circle the naming part.
Put a line under the telling part.

17. Jan has a dog.

18. Her dog digs a hole.

F. Write the words in sentence order.

19. today? Is here Hal

20. a saw pig. Sam

Synonyms

G. Write the synonym for each word in dark type.

21. Snuffy is in the **woods**.   lake   forest

22. Please **save** your paper.   keep   get

Telephone

H. Bob called Tom. Bob wanted Tom to call him at
555-7421. Sue answered the telephone. Write the
message Sue should take.

To **23.** ___	Who called? **24.** ___
Message **25.** ___	Message taken by **26.** ___

Illustration by Douglas Florian

UNIT TWO

USING LANGUAGE TO CLASSIFY

=== PART ONE ===

Unit Theme *Animals*

Language Awareness Nouns

=== PART TWO ===

Literature *A Bird Can Fly* by Douglas Florian

A Reason for Writing Classifying

Writing
IN YOUR JOURNAL

WRITER'S WARM-UP ◆ How many animals can you name? Maybe you have seen animals at a zoo, on a farm, or in a circus. You might have a pet animal or know a favorite story about an animal. Think about the animals you know and write about one of them in your journal.

Nouns for People and Places

My sister sees a zebra at the zoo.

The words **sister**, **zebra**, and **zoo** are nouns.
The noun **sister** names a person.

♦ A **noun** names a person, place, or thing.

Find each noun that names a person.
Then write the nouns.

1. A man took pictures.

2. The boy arrived next.

3. His mother followed.

4. Some children laughed.

5. The teacher held a map.

6. One girl lost her ticket.

7. Is your friend here yet?

◆ The nouns in the box name places.
Write them.

| forest | school | desert | lake | beach |

My class at __a__ learned where some animals live. My teacher showed pictures of a __b__ with many trees. Squirrels and chipmunks live there. There are many sea gulls and sand crabs at the __c__ . Camels do not need much water to live. They live in the __d__ . Turtles and fish often swim in a __e__ .

◆ Apply   Think about your neighborhood.
Write a sentence about a person and a place you know.

Nouns for Things

The hamster is in its cage.

The words **hamster** and **cage**
are nouns that name things.

◆ Copy the sentences.
Circle the nouns that name things.
Can you find 11?

1. My pet likes its wheel.

2. These seeds are for the hamster to eat.

3. There are carrots and lettuce, too.

4. Did you fill the dish with food?

5. I clean the floor of the cage with a brush.

◆ **Apply** Think of other nouns that name things.
Write a sentence with the new nouns.

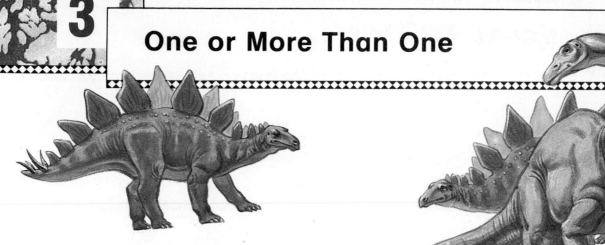

3 One or More Than One

dinosaur + s = dinosaurs

♦ Many nouns add **-s** to mean **more than one**.

1–6. Find the nouns that mean more than one. Then write them.

This animal lived many years ago. It had three horns on its head. It walked on four legs. Large plants grew all over the land. There were no roads or buildings.

Choose the correct noun for each sentence. Then write the sentences.

7. This dinosaur had a long (tail, tails)____.

8. It had many sharp (claw, claws) ____.

9. It was taller than a (house, houses) ____.

10. Scientists study all of its (bone, bones) ____.

4 Nouns That Add -es

fox + es = foxes   **bush + es = bushes**

The foxes hid in the bushes.

> ◆ Some nouns add **-es** to name **more than one.**
> These nouns end in **ss, x, ch,** or **sh**.

◆ Write the nouns. Add **-es** to mean more than one.

1. lunch   2. ax   3. dress   4. wish

◆ Copy the nouns.
Circle the nouns that add **-es** for more than one.

5. box   6. leash   7. clock   8. branch

9. bath   10. beach   11. glass   12. brush

 Apply   Change the nouns to mean more than one.
Add **-s** or **-es** to them.
Then write the new sentence.

Please put your dish and cup on the bench.

Nouns That Change Spelling

Some nouns change their spelling
to mean more than one.

One	More Than One
man	men
woman	women
child	children

One	More Than One
foot	feet
tooth	teeth
goose	geese
mouse	mice

◆ Think about the words in the charts.
Then complete the sentences.

People visit our farm all year.

Some __a__ and __b__ bring their

__c__ to see the animals. The boys and

girls splash their __d__ in the pond.

Every morning the hens and __e__ lay eggs.

Some gray __f__ live near the barn. They

chew corn with their __g__ .

6 Nouns That Show Ownership

The neck of the giraffe is very long.
The giraffe's neck is very long.

The **apostrophe** ⌐'⌐ and **s** show that
the neck belongs to the giraffe.

♦ Many nouns add **'s** to show ownership.

Think about what each animal owns.
Use **'s** to write each sentence
in a different way.

1. Did you see the stripes of the zebra?

2. The tail of the pig is short and curly.

3. The skin of the snake has scales.

4. Why is the tail of the beaver so flat?

5. The trunk of the elephant can hold water.

Apply What does your favorite animal own?
Write a sentence about it.
Use **'s** to show ownership.

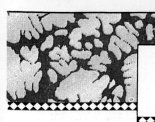

Sometimes two words are put together
to make one word.

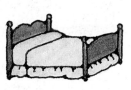 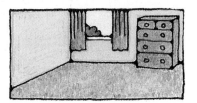 

bed + **room** = **bedroom**

◆ A word made from two words is a **compound.**

1–6. Write six compounds from these words.

paper	tea	mail	corn	ship	cup
birth	day	news	box	space	pop

Write a compound for each sentence.

7. Did you read the ___ yet?
8. Maria likes to eat ___.
9. My father's ___ is tomorrow.
10. A letter was delivered to our ___.
11. The ___ rose up into the clouds.
12. That ___ has a broken handle.

 Be a word maker.
Make up a compound for your own animal.
Draw a picture of your new animal.
Then tell about it.

rabbit + fish =
rabbitfish

Writing with Nouns

Nouns name persons, places, or things, but some nouns tell more to readers. Which sentence tells you more?

A. The animal **hops away.**
B. The rabbit **hops away.**

Both sentences name something that hops, but sentence **B** tells more. It tells what kind of animal hops. **Rabbit** is a more exact noun than **animal**. Another exact noun, such as **frog** or **kangaroo**, would give a different idea.

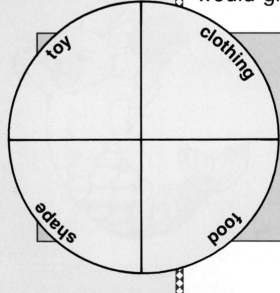

The Grammar Game ◆
Make a word wheel! Choose an exact noun for each part. Copy this wheel. Then draw your nouns.

Working Together

Work with your group. Choose exact nouns to make your writing better.

◆ Write an exact noun for each noun in ( ). Choose nouns from the list or use the group's ideas!

Nouns

soccer	lunch	beans
carrots	checkers	snack

1. We ate our (meal) at the park.
2. Ann carried (vegetables) in a bag.
3. Later we played some (game).

◆ Agree on an exact noun for each sentence. Write your group's story.

I went to the ___ . My ___ went with me. We rode on a ___ . We saw many ___ .

In Your Group

- ♦ Give everyone a turn to share.
- ♦ Listen when others talk.
- ♦ Agree or disagree in a nice way.

ROOSTER
sculpture by Gregorio Marzan
El Museo del Barrio
Photograph courtesy of the
Corcoran Gallery of Art.

STRIPED GIRAFFE
sculpture by Gregorio Marzan
El Museo del Barrio
Photograph courtesy of the
Corcoran Gallery of Art.

ZEBRA
sculpture by David Alvarez
Collection of the Museum of
American Folk Art,
Gift of Elizabeth Wechter.

UNIT TWO

USING LANGUAGE
TO
CLASSIFY

=== **PART TWO** ===

Literature *A Bird Can Fly* **by Douglas Florian**

A Reason for Writing Classifying

CREATIVE
Writing

FINE ARTS ◆ Look at the animals at the left.
What might the animals say if they could
speak? Give each animal a name. Then write
what each animal might say to you. If you
like, write what you would say to the animal.

A Strategy for Classifying

A Question Wheel

Do you ever wonder about things? That's good! When you wonder, you ask questions. When you ask questions, you learn things.

◆ Look at this picture of a bird. What do you you wonder about a bird? Read the question. Can you think of other questions to ask? Tell your questions. Do you know some answers? Can you find out?

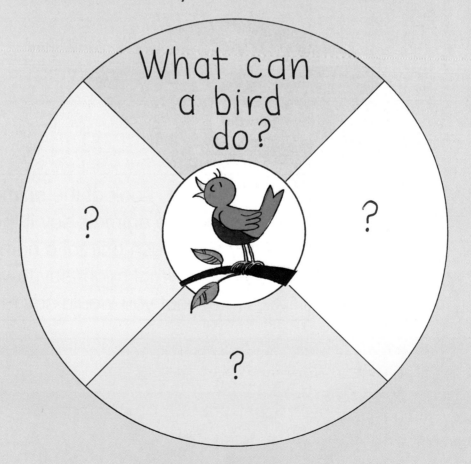

◆ Now draw a circle. Inside the circle, draw an animal you like. Make spaces for four questions on the outside. In one space write "What can (your animal) do?"

◆ Work with a partner. Talk about what your animals can do. Think of other questions to ask about your animals.

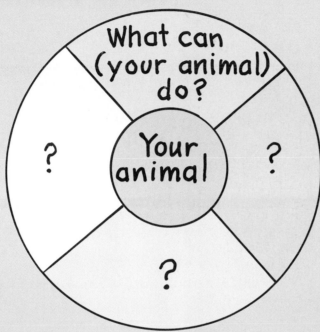

Next you will read *A Bird Can Fly*. Think of some questions about what animals can do. As you read, look for some answers to the questions.

♦ What questions did you think of about your animal?

♦ When do you ask questions?

LITERATURE

A BIRD CAN FLY
by Douglas Florian

A bird can fly.
A bird can sing.
A bird can build a nest.

But a bird can't build a dam.
A beaver can build a dam.

A beaver can cut down trees with its teeth.
A beaver can live underwater for fifteen minutes.

But a beaver can't live underground.
An ant can live underground.

An ant can walk upside down on a branch.
An ant can carry five times its own weight.

But an ant can't carry a boy on its back.
A tortoise can carry a boy on its back.

A tortoise can live
in a shell.
A tortoise can pull its tail
into its shell.

But a tortoise can't hang by its tail.
A monkey can hang by its tail.

A monkey can live in a tree.
A monkey can travel through the jungle.

But a monkey can't travel across the desert.
A camel can travel across the desert.

A camel can store food
in its body.
A camel can drink twenty
gallons of water.

But a camel can't breathe
underwater.
A fish can breathe
underwater.

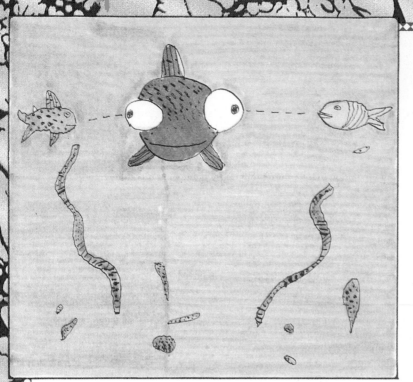

A fish can see things on both sides
of its head at the same time.
A fish can swim great distances.

But a fish can't fly.
A bird can fly.

Library Link ♦ *If you liked reading this
story, look for the book* Nature Walk, *also by
Douglas Florian.*

 Reader's Response

Which animal did you like best? Tell why.

A BIRD CAN FLY

 ## Responding to Literature

1. What can you do that your favorite animal cannot do? What can the animal do?

2. Draw your favorite animal for a class mural. Write a sound your animal makes.

3. How many things can you do? Make a giant list of all the things the boys and girls in your class can do.

 ## Writing to Learn

Think and Wonder ♦ Draw a surprise animal that no one has ever seen before. Draw it in the middle of a question wheel. What can it do?

Question Wheel

Write ♦ What questions could you ask your animal? Write them in your wheel.

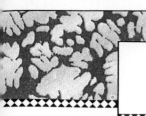

STUDY SKILLS ♦
ABC Order

The letters of the alphabet are in **ABC order.**
Many lists of words or names are in ABC order.
ABC order helps you find words or names quickly.

Words in a dictionary are
listed in ABC order.
Telephone books and other lists
may be in this order, too.

ant
Bb beaver
Cc camel

ABCDEFGHIJKLMNOPQRSTUVWXYZ
a b c d e f g h i j k l m n o p q r s t u v w x y z

◆ Practice ABC order. Write each group of letters.
Then write the missing letters.

1. __ KL   4. __ pq   7. EF __   10. __ t __

2. FG __   5. rs __   8. __ XY   11. __ C __

3. U __ W   6. m __ o   9. GH __   12. __ w __

◆ Write each group of letters that is in ABC order.

13. lkm suy   16. afe hjt   19. PQS MON

14. drw bnm   17. twx fej   20. LQP HKL

15. orq gik   18. dgh ywx   21. CGI RTQ

Look at the first letter of each word.
Use the first letter to write each group of
words in ABC order.

22. pig
    cow
    fox

23. wing
    fin
    tail
    beak

24. fly
    swim
    walk
    climb

25. quack
    bark
    moo

26. den
    pond
    nest
    shell

27. hen
    goose
    monkey
    dog

28. Muffin
    Peaches
    Brownie

29. lion
    horse
    rabbit
    tiger

30. paw
    hoof
    claw
    foot

31. hair
    fur
    skin

32. squeak
    cluck
    peep
    buzz

33. Rusty
    Mittens
    Spot
    Feather

Apply Find the names of the seven animals
in *A Bird Can Fly*. Write them in ABC order.
Hint: **Beaver** comes before **bird**.

A dictionary page has **entry words** in dark type.
A dictionary gives a meaning for each word.
Some entry words have more than one meaning. Entry
words are always in ABC order.

Two **guide words** are at the top of each page. The
first guide word tells the first entry word on that page.
The second guide word tells the last word on the page.

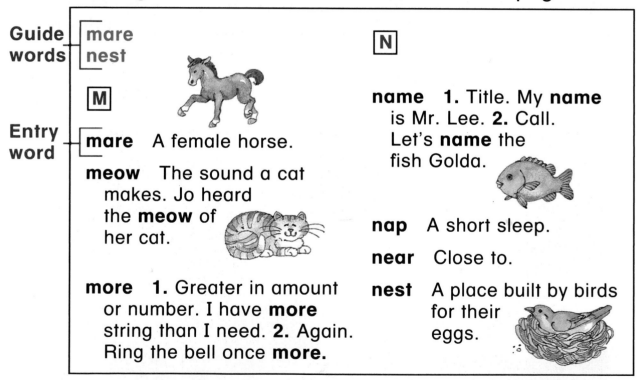

Guide words
mare
nest

Entry word

M

mare   A female horse.

meow   The sound a cat
makes. Jo heard
the **meow** of
her cat.

more   1. Greater in amount
or number. I have **more**
string than I need. 2. Again.
Ring the bell once **more.**

N

name   1. Title. My **name**
is Mr. Lee. 2. Call.
Let's **name** the
fish Golda.

nap   A short sleep.

near   Close to.

nest   A place built by birds
for their
eggs.

◆ Read the entry for **more**. Write the number of the
meaning that goes with each sentence below.

1. Walk the dog once **more**.   **2.** He needs **more** water.

◆ Put the words in ABC order. Look at the second letter.

3. cub
colt
calf

5. wing
water
wood

4. feed
farm
fly

6. pig
puppy
pony

◆ Look at each pair of guide words. Write the entry word from the box that will be on the same page.

| giraffe | eel | lion | bee | owl | toad |

7. **bat**
bird

9. **tiger**
tree

11. **fox**
goat

8. **eagle**
elephant

10. **lamb**
llama

12. **otter**
owl

Apply Look up the name of your favorite animal in a dictionary. Write the guide words that are on that page.

Using the Word Finder

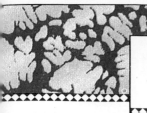

A Word Finder begins on page 323 of this book. It lists words together that are synonyms. The entries are in ABC order.

◆ Read this entry for **go.**

go ◆	to move to or from something. We <u>go</u> to the store.
fly	to move in the air using wings. I saw a jet <u>fly</u> in the sky.
jump	to leap up or leap over something. The horses <u>jump</u> over the fence.
ride	to move in or on something. We <u>ride</u> in a train to the city.
run	to go faster than walking. We can <u>run</u> until our legs hurt.
walk	to move one foot in front of the other. When I <u>walk</u>, I look at everything.

An eagle can go high in the sky.
An eagle can fly high in the sky.

The word **fly** is a better way to tell how an eagle moves.

◆ Write a better word for **go** in each sentence below.

1. Watch the frog **go** to that rock.
2. A horse can **go** faster than a cow.
3. Let my cat **go** in the wagon.

Read this story that Paula wrote about ants.

Uncle Fred gave me an ant farm. He had an ant farm when he was little. Mom built a shelf for it. She put the shelf up high. My dog is too little to see it. I like to watch the ants. These little insects work all day long.

Find the word **little** in the Word Finder that begins on page 323. Write a better word for **little** for each blank in Paula's story.

Uncle Fred gave me an ant farm. He had an ant farm when he was __a__ . Mom built a shelf for it. She put the shelf up high. My dog is too __b__ to see it. I like to watch the ants. These __c__ insects work all day long.

Apply Write a sentence with the word **happy**. Now find **happy** in the Word Finder. Write your sentence again. Use a better word for **happy**.

Writing a Book Page

You have read *A Bird Can Fly*. You learned many things animals can do. You also learned some things they cannot do.

Now you will write about an animal. You will make a page for a book about animals. You will tell what your animal can do. You will also tell what it cannot do. Later you can share your book with another class.

1 Prewriting

First you have to choose a topic. What animal will you write about? Then you will gather ideas about your topic.

Choose Your Topic ◆ With your classmates, talk about kinds of animals. Think of animals that fly, swim, walk, or crawl. They might be pets or farm animals. They might be wild animals or animals in a zoo. List the names on the chalkboard.

Read the list. Then write down your favorite animals from the list. Choose one to write about. Choose the one you like best. Circle your choice.

My Favorite Animals

eagle

whale

giraffe

cobra

Choose Your Plan ♦ Here are two ways to get ideas. Try the one you like better.

PREWRITING IDEAS

Plan One ♦ Question Wheel

Make a question wheel. Draw your animal in the middle. Write questions around the outside. One question might be "What can it do?" Another question might be "What can it <u>not</u> do?" You might ask "Where does it live?" You might ask "How does it move around?" Write the questions you want to ask. Think about the answers you already know.

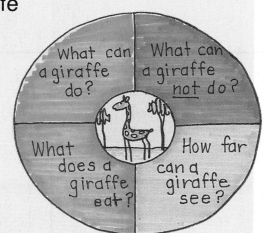

Plan Two ♦ A Two-Sided Chart

Write the name of your animal. Then fold your paper to make two sides. On one side write things your animal can do. On the other write things it cannot do.

a giraffe

<u>can</u>	<u>can not</u>
run	fly
see a long way	climb
eat high leaves	sing

2 Writing

Put your prewriting notes in front of you. Did you make a question wheel? Did you make a two-sided chart? Look at what you wrote.

Now write some sentences about your animal. Tell what the animal can do. Also tell what it cannot do.

3 Revising

Read what Jesse wrote. He fixed a noun mistake. He had written a noun showing ownership. That was not what he meant. He also added a word.

Giraffes
~~Giraffe's~~ can see very far. they can ⋀ easily reach high leafs. Giraffes cannot climb.

REVISING IDEA

Read your sentences to yourself. See if you want to make changes. Then read your sentences to a partner. Talk about ways you might make your writing better.

◆ Did I tell what my animal can do? Did I tell what it cannot do?

◆ Should I add or change any words?

Grammar Check ◆ Did I use exact nouns in my sentence?

4 Proofreading

Proofread your sentences to fix mistakes. These questions can help you proofread.

- ◆ Did I spell each word correctly?

- ◆ Did I use capital letters correctly?

- ◆ Did I use the correct mark at the end of each sentence?

Giraffe's can see very far. they can reach high leafs. Giraffes cannot climb.

Make sure your sentences are correct. Then get ready to copy them onto your book page. You will make your book page next.

5 Publishing

Now make your book page. Draw a picture of your animal. Neatly copy your sentences below the picture.

Here are two ways you can share your book page.

PUBLISHING IDEAS

Share Aloud

Play a guessing game. Read your sentences aloud. Leave out your animal's name. Ask your listeners to guess its name. Then show your picture to the class.

Giraffes can see very far.
They can easily reach high leaves.
Giraffes can not climb.

Share in Writing

With your classmates, make a book about animals. Put all the animal pages in ABC order. Let another class borrow your book. Ask each reader to write a sentence. The sentence should tell one thing the reader learned. Ask your readers to send their sentences back with your book.

CURRICULUM ◆CONNECTION◆

Writing for Science

When you classify you put things in groups. You find out which things belong together and why. In science you do this often. As you classify things you learn about them. Writing will help you do it.

Writing to Learn

Think and Wonder ◆ This animal has a strange name. It is a bongo. Think like a scientist. What do you want to know about a bongo? What questions do you have? Make a question wheel about a bongo.

Write ◆ Try to write the answer to one of your questions.

Writing in Your Journal

You have read about many different animals in this unit. What is your favorite? Write about an animal you like or one you would like to know more about.

bongo

Question Wheel

BOOKS TO ENJOY

Read More About It

Q Is for Duck
by Mary Elting and Michael Folsom
This alphabet guessing game is all about animals. You will have fun trying to guess the riddles. Can you guess why Q is for Duck?

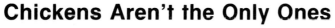

Chickens Aren't the Only Ones
by Ruth Heller
Did you know that many animals lay eggs? Find out about it in this book.
New York Academy of Sciences Book Award

Book Report Idea   Poster

You can put books in groups like a library does. Make a poster for a book you like. Write the title and author. Tell what the book is about and draw a picture. Then discuss which books go together. Help your class put the posters in groups. Put each group in a folder or on a bulletin board.

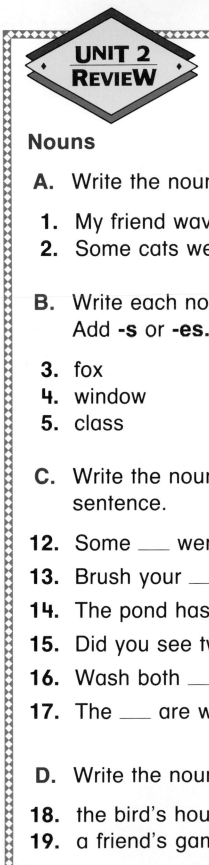

Nouns

A. Write the nouns in each sentence.

1. My friend waved from the car.
2. Some cats went into the house.

B. Write each noun to mean more than one.
Add **-s** or **-es.**

3. fox
4. window
5. class

6. bee
7. bench
8. flower

9. brush
10. ax
11. sister

C. Write the noun that means more than one for each sentence.

12. Some ___ went home.   **a.** child   **b.** children
13. Brush your ___ .   **a.** teeth   **b.** tooth
14. The pond has many ___ .   **a.** geese   **b.** goose
15. Did you see two ___ ?   **a.** men   **b.** man
16. Wash both ___ .   **a.** feet   **b.** foot
17. The ___ are working.   **a.** woman   **b.** women

D. Write the nouns that show ownership.

18. the bird's house
19. a friend's game

20. my sister's book
21. his pet's toy

Compound Words

E. Match the words to make compound words.

22. sail   **a.** shoe   **25.** rain   **d.** ball
23. class   **b.** boat   **26.** basket   **e.** lace
24. horse   **c.** room   **27.** shoe   **f.** drop

ABC Order

F. Write each group of words in ABC order.

28. put   big   well   **29.** say   look   cold

Word Finder

G. Read the entry below for **make**.

make	to cause something to be or to happen. Sally can <u>make</u> lunch for herself.
build	to construct something from materials. Let's <u>build</u> a wooden clubhouse.
create	to think up something new. Can you <u>create</u> a new game?

Now read each sentence. Write a better word for **make**.

30. **Make** a new design for your book cover.
31. Can Donna **make** a chair with wood?

Illustration by Molly Bang

UNIT THREE

USING LANGUAGE TO IMAGINE

=== PART ONE ===

Unit Theme   *World of Make-Believe*

Language Awareness   Verbs

=== PART TWO ===

Literature   *The Paper Crane* **by Molly Bang**

A Reason for Writing   Imagining

Writing
IN YOUR JOURNAL

WRITER'S WARM-UP ◆ When you close your eyes and imagine, what wonderful things do you see? When you make believe, you can meet people and animals from different places and different times. Write in your journal about your favorite make-believe story.

Verbs

We dance on the stage.

The word **dance** is a verb.
It tells what we do.

◆ A word that shows action is a **verb.**

Find the verb in each sentence.
Then write each verb.

1. Paul and Emily sing together.

2. Uncle John and Aunt Meg help us.

3. They sew funny costumes.

4. I play the drum loudly.

5. We give programs to everyone.

6. My friends clap hard.

◆ Write the verbs for the story.

visit   wear   watch
learn   fold

Our friends Mr. and Mrs. Tanaka
__a__ us often. Today they __b__ some
paper into hats. My brother and I __c__
carefully. Then we __d__ the secret. Now
we __e__ different hats every day.

Apply Think about a special hat.
Write what you do when you wear that hat.
Then draw a line under the verb.

2 Adding -s to Verbs

One girl reads. **Two girls read.**

◆ Add **-s** to a verb to tell about one person or thing.

◆ Add **-s** to some of the verbs in ( ).

1. Three pigs (work) ___ on their houses.

2. The little red hen (work) ___ hard.

3. Rapunzel (throw) ___ her hair down.

4. Hansel and Gretel (throw) ___ crumbs.

5. Pinocchio (want) ___ a shorter nose.

6. Three little kittens (want) ___ mittens.

Apply Think of some verbs for these sentences. Write as many sentences as you can.

Goldilocks ___. The three bears ___.

3

Adding *-ed* to Verbs

climb + ed = climbed
Jack climbed the beanstalk.

♦ Many verbs that tell about the past
end with **-ed**.

Add **-ed** to the verbs in ( ).

Jack (discover) **a** the treasure.

The giant (shout) **b** . Jack (act) **c**

quickly. He (start) **d** down the beanstalk.

The giant (follow) **e** . Jack

(jump) **f** off. Then the beanstalk

(crash) **g** . What

(happen) **h** next? The

giant never (bother) **i**

Jack again.

4

Adding *-s* and *-ed* to Verbs

◆ Add **-s** or **-ed** to the words in ( ).

1. Long ago children (enjoy) ___ stories by candlelight.

2. Today a computer (print) ___ my stories.

3. Now it (add) ___ pictures for each page.

4. Last week the librarian (talk) ___ about fairy tales.

5. Then we (listen) ___ to a story tape.

6. After that we (borrow) ___ three books.

7. Now my sister (want) ___ another book.

tied   untied

Prefix	Meaning	Example
re-	again	re + read = reread
un-	not	un + wrap = unwrap

◆ A **prefix** is a letter or letters added to the beginning of a word.

◆ Write the two words that have prefixes in each sentence.

1. Tony will rebuild the unsafe steps.

2. We are unsure how to rewrite the play.

3. Sue unsnaps and refolds her torn costume.

4. She is unhappy that she must resew it.

◆ 5–6. Rewrite the sentence two ways.
Add **re-** or **un-** to the word in dark type.
Tell how the meaning of the sentence changes.

Let's **pack** this trunk.

Writing with Verbs

Verbs show actions, but some verbs tell more to readers. Which sentence below gives more information?

A. Sam looked at the purple cow.
B. Sam stared at the purple cow.

Both sentences tell that Sam saw something strange, but sentence **B** tells more. It tells how Sam looked at the cow. **Stared** is a more exact verb than **looked**. How would the meaning change if Sam **peeked** at the cow?

The Grammar Game ◆ What do you do?
Add two exact verbs to each list. Then pick a partner and act out a verb from each list. Can you guess each verb?

At Home	At School	Outside
sleep	**talk**	**move**

Working Together

Work with your group. Choose exact verbs to tell more in your sentences.

◆ Write more exact verbs for the words in dark type. Use verbs from the list or other ideas from your group.

nibbled	**yelled**
marched	**floated**

1. "Help me!" I **said**.
2. A fluffy cloud **went** by.
3. The giraffe **ate** leaves.
4. She **walked** away.

♦ WORD FINDER ♦

Read the story. Then find **get** in the Word Finder that begins on page 323. Try to use **get** and each of the other words in the story. Write the verbs your group chooses.

  If I __a__ the biggest fish, I will __b__ first prize! How can I __c__ a pole? I better save money to __d__ one.

THE UNICORN IN CAPTIVITY
Franco-Flemish tapestry
The Metropolitan Museum of Art,
Gift of John D. Rockefeller, Jr.
The Cloisters Collection, 1937.

UNIT THREE

USING LANGUAGE
TO
IMAGINE

=== **PART TWO** ===

Literature *The Paper Crane* **by Molly Bang**

A Reason for Writing Imagining

CREATIVE
Writing

FINE ARTS ◆ Unicorns are make-believe animals. They look like horses, but they have one long horn. Imagine that you could walk up to the fence in the picture. What would you like to ask the unicorn? Write the questions you would ask.

CRITICAL THINKING ◆
A Strategy for Imagining

A Conclusion Sentence

Did someone ever help you do something? Did you decide that person was nice? If you did, you drew a conclusion. You decided what you thought about that person.

What can help you draw a conclusion about someone? Think about how the person acts. Actions can help you draw a conclusion about a person.

◆ Look at the girl in this picture. What is she doing? Draw a conclusion about her. Finish the sentence below the picture.

I think the girl is ___ .

◆ Read this story. Look at the pictures.
Draw conclusions about Rachel and Paul.
Finish the sentences below the pictures.

Rachel and Paul went on a picnic.
Rachel forgot to bring her lunch. Paul
gave Rachel half of his sandwich.

I think Rachel is ___ .

I think Paul is ___ .

Next you will read *The Paper Crane*. In
the story, one stranger gives another a
gift. Draw conclusions about these people.

◆ How did you decide what you thought
about Rachel? About Paul?

◆ Is it ever important to draw a conclusion
about someone? Why?

LITERATURE

The Paper Crane

MOLLY BANG

A man once owned
a restaurant
on a busy road.
He loved to cook
good food and
he loved to serve it.
He worked from
morning until night,
and he was happy.

But a new highway was built close by.
Travelers drove straight from one place to another
and no longer stopped at the restaurant.
Many days went by when no guests came at all.
The man became very poor, and had nothing to do
but dust and polish his empty plates and tables.

LITERATURE: Story

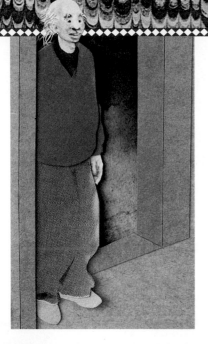

One evening a stranger
came into the restaurant.
His clothes were old and worn,
but he had an unusual, gentle manner.

Though he said he had no money
to pay for food,
the owner invited him to sit down.
He cooked the best meal he could make
and served him like a king.

When the stranger had finished, he said to his host,
''I cannot pay you with money, but I would like to thank you
in my own way.'' He picked up a paper napkin from
the table and folded it into the shape of a crane.
''You have only to clap your hands,'' he said,
''and this bird will come to life and dance for you.
Take it, and enjoy it while it is with you.''
With these words the stranger left.

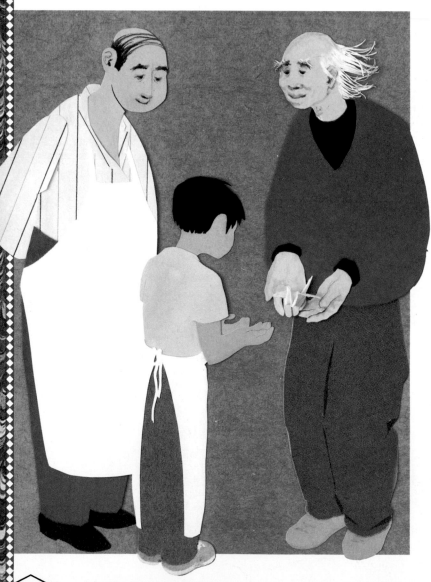

LITERATURE: Story

It happened just as the stranger had said.
The owner had only to clap his hands
and the paper crane became a
living bird, flew down to
the floor, and danced.

Soon word of the dancing
crane spread, and people
came from far and near
to see the magic bird
perform.

The owner was happy again, for his restaurant was always full of guests. He cooked and served and had company from morning until night.

The weeks passed. And the months.

One evening a man came into the restaurant.
His clothes were old and worn,
but he had an unusual, gentle manner.
The owner knew him at once and was overjoyed.

The stranger, however, said nothing.
He took a flute from his pocket,
raised it to his lips, and began to play.

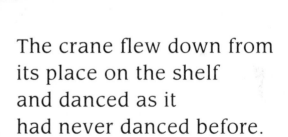

The crane flew down from
its place on the shelf
and danced as it
had never danced before.

The stranger finished
playing, lowered the flute
from his lips,
and returned it
to his pocket.
He climbed on the back of
the crane, and they flew out
of the door and away.

The restaurant still stands by the side of the road,
and guests still come to eat the good food
and hear the story of the gentle stranger
and the magic crane made from a paper napkin.
But neither the stranger nor the dancing crane
has ever been seen again.

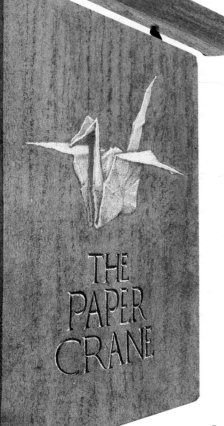

THE
PAPER
CRANE

Library Link ◆ *If you enjoyed this folktale
by Molly Bang, you might like to read her
Japanese fairy tale,* Dawn.

Reader's Response

Would you like to fly away on a magic crane?
Tell why or why not.

The Paper Crane

Responding to Literature

1. Can you dance like a crane? Try it. Flap your arms. Hop. Add some other actions.

2. The stranger gave a gift by making the crane dance. Laughter and friendship are gifts. What other gifts are not in boxes?

3. Make believe your favorite toy could come to life. Tell what it could do.

Writing to Learn

Think and Decide ◆ Do you know someone who needs some help? Tell why you want to help. Then decide how you can help that person.

I think I should help Mr. Jenkins because he helps us every day.

Conclusion Sentence

Write ◆ Now finish your chart. Add a sentence that says, I think I should help ___ because ___ .

SPEAKING and LISTENING ◆
Telling a Story in Order

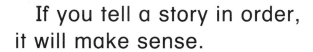

If you tell a story in order, it will make sense.

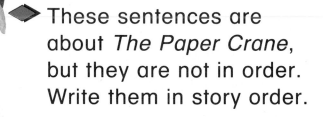 These sentences are about *The Paper Crane*, but they are not in order. Write them in story order.

- ◆ The paper crane came alive when the owner clapped.

- ◆ Travelers stopped coming to the restaurant.

- ◆ The owner was happy, for he had many guests again.

- ◆ The stranger folded a napkin into a paper crane.

Now tell the story of *The Paper Crane* in your own words.

Apply What is your favorite story?
Share it with a partner.
Tell all the parts in story order.

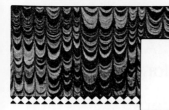

Every story needs a good ending. The ending tells you how the story turns out. It answers the reader's questions.

◆ Write a new ending for *The Paper Crane.* Here are some ideas:

- ♦ Suppose the owner had not served the stranger.

- ♦ Imagine if the paper crane had not come alive.

- ♦ Perhaps the stranger never came back.

When you write, use one of these ideas or make up your own.

 Copy this story on a piece of paper.

Rae found an old paper. It looked like a strange map. She followed the steps. Soon she came to a stone walk. The map had an X near the top.

Now write an ending for the story. Draw a picture for it.

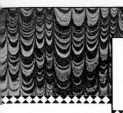

SPEAKING ♦
Acting Out a Story

Setting: A small village, long ago

Characters:

Narrator	Anna
Mother	Felix
Old Woman	Edgar
Maude	Mayor

The Magic Porridge Pot
a play adapted from a traditional tale

Narrator: Anna and her mother were very poor. They lived in a tiny house at the edge of a small village.

Mother: I'm sorry, my child. We have no food.

Anna: Don't worry, Mother. I will go to the forest. Maybe I'll find some nuts or berries for us.

Narrator: Anna searched for food, but she had no luck. Soon, she sat on a rock and began to cry.

Anna: What shall I do? I'm so very hungry!

Old Woman: I shall help you, little girl.

Anna: Who are you?

Old Woman: Never mind that. Here is a magic kettle. Take it home and put it on the fire. Say *Cook, good kettle, cook!* It will fill up with porridge. When you've had enough to eat, you must say, *Stop, good kettle, stop!* Then, and only then, will the magic kettle stop cooking.

Anna: Oh, thank you, thank you!

Old Woman: Take fair warning. Remember the magic words!

Narrator: Anna ran home and put the kettle on.

Mother: Have you found food for us, Anna?

Anna: Watch, Mother! Cook, good kettle, cook!

Mother:	My heavens! Look at all the porridge!
Narrator:	Anna and her mother ate until they were full.
Anna:	Stop, good kettle, stop!
Narrator:	And it did. Now Anna and her mother had plenty to eat. The next day, Anna visited her friend Maude. While Anna was out, her mother got hungry.
Mother:	Cook, good kettle, cook!
Narrator:	As usual, porridge appeared. But the mother forgot the magic words to make the kettle stop.
Mother:	Okay, that's enough porridge.
Narrator:	Porridge spilled over the kettle, and out the door. It ran down the village street.
Mother:	Please, kettle, quit!
Felix:	Oh, my! Look at all the porridge!
Edgar:	I think it must be a porridge flood!
Mother:	Help, help! Kettle, please stop cooking!
Maude:	Anna, it's your mother and a flood of porridge!
Felix:	Cut it out, kettle!
Maude:	No more porridge, kettle!
Mayor:	I order you to stop, kettle!
Anna:	Thank you, friends, but *I* must do it.
Narrator:	Anna ran home through puddles of porridge. When she got to the tiny house, she said . . .
Anna:	Stop, good kettle, stop.
Narrator:	And it did.

Apply Take turns acting out the story.

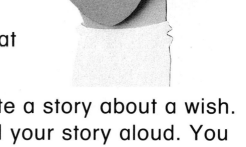

WRITING PROCESS
IMAGING

Writing a Story

Magic happened in the story *The Paper Crane*. A paper crane came to life. What if magic things happened in real life? Can you imagine it? What magic thing would you wish for? Would you wish that pizza grew on trees? Would you wish that you could fly?

Now you will write a story about a wish. Later you can read your story aloud. You can also help make a book of stories.

1 Prewriting

First get ready to write your story. Choose your topic and gather your ideas.

Choose Your Topic ♦ People say four-leaf clovers bring good luck. Draw a four-leaf clover. In each leaf, write one wish. Draw a star next to the wish you like best.

I wish I could be invisible for a day.

I wish my bicycle could fly.

I wish I could ride on a spaceship.

I wish my cat could sing. ✹

Choose Your Plan ◆ Here are two plans for gathering story ideas. Use the plan that you like better.

Plan One ◆ A Conclusion Sentence

Think about your wish. What would happen if it came true?

Draw a picture. Show what would happen if your wish came true. Then write a conclusion sentence under the picture. Your sentence should begin like this:

If my wish came true, I think ___ .

If my wish came true, I think my cat would be on T.V.

Plan Two ◆ A Story Order Chart

Make a chart to help plan your story. Make three boxes. Write your wish in the "First" box. Then think. What would happen if your wish came true? Write notes about it in the "Next" box. Then think again. How would the story end? Write notes about it in the "Last" box.

First
My cat starts to sing!

Next I'm surprised. People come to hear the songs. We go on T.V.

Last We are famous. We put on shows.

2 Writing

Put your prewriting picture or chart in front of you. Then begin to write your story. Here are some ways you might begin.

- ◆ Once I wished that . . . .
- ◆ I didn't believe in magic until . . . .

After you start, tell your story in order. What happened after your wish came true? Then what happened? What happened last?

As you write, don't worry about spelling. You can fix mistakes later. Just think about writing a good story.

3 Revising

Look at how Rosa revised her story. She added some words. She used a more exact verb.

One day I wished ∧ my cat Susie would sing. then she sang! People came ran to hear her. Then we went on TV. Now we put on shows evywhere!

REVISING IDEA

Read your story to yourself. Then read it aloud to a partner. Talk about ways to make your writing better.

◆ Did I tell my story in the right order?

◆ Did I make all the details clear?

Grammar Check ◆ Did I use exact verbs?

Now revise your story. Make changes you think will make it better.

4 Proofreading

Now fix any mistakes. These questions may help you find them.

♦ Did I spell each word correctly?

♦ Did I use capital letters correctly?

♦ Did I use the correct mark at the end of each sentence?

Now add a title. Then make a neat copy of your story.

PROOFREADING MARKS

◯ check spelling

≡ capital letter

One day I wished ^(my cat) Susie would sing. ≡then she sang! People came ^(ran) to hear her. Then we went on TV. Now we put on shows (evywhere) everywhere!

5 Publishing

Here are two ways to share your story.

PUBLISHING IDEAS

Share Aloud

Make a story circle with three classmates. Take turns reading your stories aloud. Ask each listener to draw a picture about your story.

Share in Writing

Make a classroom book called *Magic Wishes*. Put all your stories in the book. During free time, read and enjoy the stories. Tell the writers what you liked best in their stories.

My Magic Wish
One day I wished my cat Susie would sing. Then she sang! People ran to hear her. Then we went on TV. Now we put on shows everywhere!

Writing for Social Studies

In social studies you learn about people in other lands. Many of them may live in places that are very different from yours. You can make those people and places seem real to you. How? The secret is to imagine. Imagine, and then write.

Writing to Learn

Think and Decide ◆ Look at the picture and imagine. What is this person like? What is he thinking and feeling? What is it like to live here? Think about it.

Write ◆ Write a conclusion sentence to tell what you decide.

I think _____.

Conclusion Sentence

Writing in Your Journal

You have read about many make-believe people in this unit. Write what you would say to your favorite make-believe character.

BOOKS TO ENJOY

 ## Read More About It

The Star Maiden
by Barbara Juster Esbensen
The Ojibway people tell this beautiful tale about the brightest star in the sky.

A Story, A Story
by Gail E. Haley
This African folk tale tells you about Ananse, the Spider man, and his golden box of stories.

Caldecott Medal

 ## Book Report Idea   TV Report

Imagine that you are on a children's TV show. Tell about a book you know children will like. You can make a cardboard or paper frame to look like a TV set. Hold it in front of your face as you give your book talk.

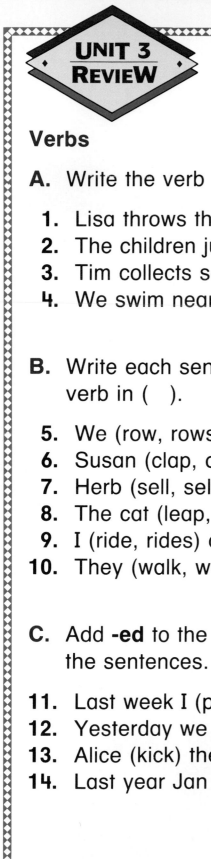

Verbs

A. Write the verb in each sentence.

1. Lisa throws the ball.
2. The children jump into the water.
3. Tim collects some shells.
4. We swim near the shore.

B. Write each sentence. Use the correct verb in (   ).

5. We (row, rows) the boat.
6. Susan (clap, claps) loudly.
7. Herb (sell, sells) newspapers.
8. The cat (leap, leaps) up.
9. I (ride, rides) on a bus.
10. They (walk, walks) together.

C. Add **-ed** to the verbs in (   ). Write the sentences. Use the new verbs.

11. Last week I (pick) some apples.
12. Yesterday we (march) in music class.
13. Alice (kick) the soccer ball.
14. Last year Jan (clean) the garage.

Prefixes

D. Write each sentence. Put a line under the words that have prefixes.

15. Mike untied his shoe.

16. Please replay the song.

17. Can you unlock the door?

18. I will wash the unbroken cup.

19. Did Kate rewrite her poem?

20. Will you rewrap the package?

21. Jake unplugged the toaster.

22. Kim refilled the pitcher.

Stories

E. Write these sentences in story order.

23. She fixed Andy's skate.

24. Andy was skating.

25. A wheel fell off his skate.

26. Mom got some tools.

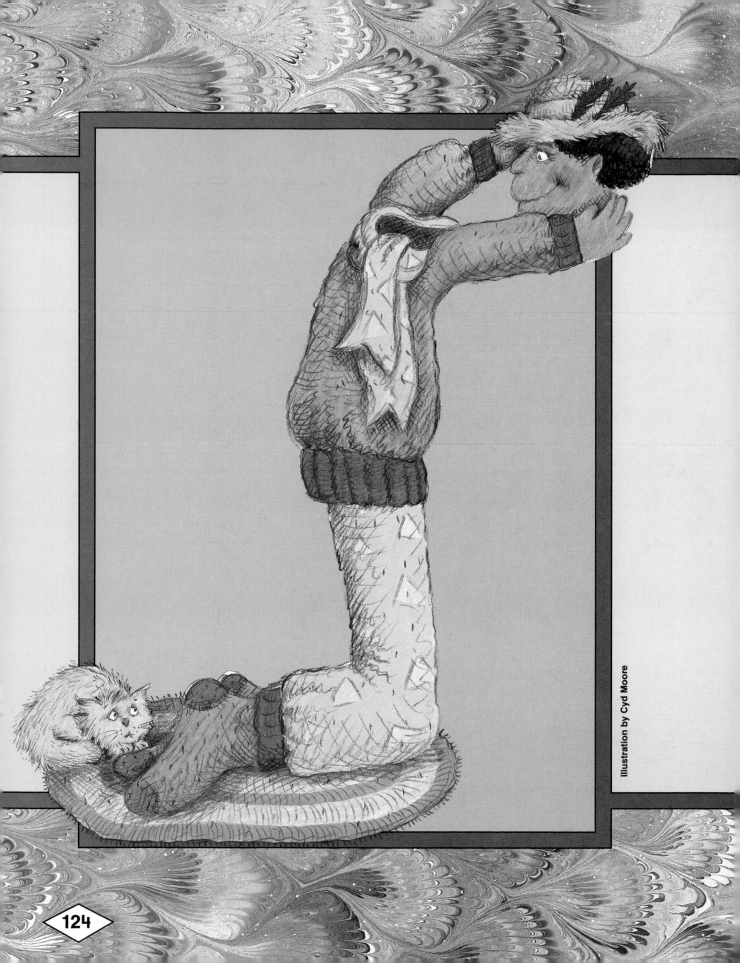

Illustration by Cyd Moore

UNIT FOUR

USING LANGUAGE
TO
CREATE

===== **PART ONE** =====

Unit Theme *Humor*

Language Awareness Adjectives

===== **PART TWO** =====

Literature Poetry

A Reason for Writing Creating

Writing
IN YOUR JOURNAL

WRITER'S WARM-UP ◆ All of us have a sense of humor. You may know some funny jokes and riddles. What else makes you smile and laugh? Write in your journal about something that you think is funny or silly.

1 Adjectives

We are making puppets.
We are making funny puppets.

The word **puppet** is a noun.
The adjective **funny** tells more about the noun.

♦ An **adjective** tells more about a noun.

Copy the sentences below.
Put a line under the nouns.
Circle the adjectives that tell
more about the nouns.

1. Mine has green hair.

2. It looks like a big frog.

3. I put soft heads on it.

4. She made a silly monster.

5. It has furry arms.

6. She put square eyes on it.

7. Another is wearing high boots.

8. It has them on short legs.

9. Yours has a tiny hat.

10. They are wonderful puppets.

◆ Copy the story.
Write the best adjective for each noun.

orange	real	blue	wet
short	dirty	round	spicy

We are planning a **a** play. The **b** drum could be a **c** table for our puppets. Pam and Mark found **d** shoelaces to use for spaghetti. Then Andy put **e** paint on them. It doesn't smell like **f** sauce. It feels like **g** string. Do you think it looks like **h** food?

Apply Write about a funny puppet you could make. Use adjectives to tell what it looks like.

2 Words That Tell *How Many*

It snowed for three days.
We missed some days of school.

The words **three** and **some** tell how many.

Copy the sentences below.
Circle the words below that tell how many.

1. Saturday we had two inches of snow.

2. Then it snowed many inches on Sunday.

3. Monday six inches fell.

4. Tuesday some plows cleared our street.

5. We saw one car get stuck.

6. Then two people tried to push it.

7. Finally four people helped it get out.

8. When it snows, many cars get stuck.

9. We shoveled our sidewalk for three days.

10. It took us eight hours.

one
two
three
four
five
six
seven
eight
nine
ten

◆ Find the number words for the nouns.
Then write them for the sentences.

Tuesday __a__ children walked to the store.

We each carried __b__ bags home with us. At the

pond, __c__ people were skating. A huge snowman

had __d__ birds sitting on it. Then we saw a

snow castle with __e__ flags. When we got

home, we left __f__ boots at the door.

Apply What do you like to do with your friends
after school? Write a sentence about it.
Use some words that tell how many.

Words That Tell *What Kind*

red	black
blue	yellow
green	white
brown	orange

◆ Help make a rainbow salad.
Write the color word for each sentence.

First we cut circles of __a__ carrots.

Then we sliced __b__ and __c__ apples.

The __d__ bananas looked so sunny. Some __e__

cottage cheese was nice on the __f__ plate. We

decorated it with pieces of __g__ olives. Finally we

added __h__ nuts around the edge.

◆ Draw a shape using food.
It can be pretty or silly.
Then write a sentence
describing your shape.
Remember to use color
words in your description.

◆ Write the best adjective for each noun.
Look carefully at the pictures first.

tall
large
pointed
round
small
square
flat

Our building has a craft room. We made robots with

special blocks. Marcy made one with all __a__ blocks.

Al used __b__ blocks. Jay used __c__ pieces. Jay's

and Marcy's robots had __d__ heads. Jay's __e__ robot

was much bigger than Marcy's __f__ one. Jana's robot

had a __g__ head.

◆ Apply   Describe one of the robots in the picture.
Use color words as well as words for size and shape.
Have a friend guess which robot you are describing.

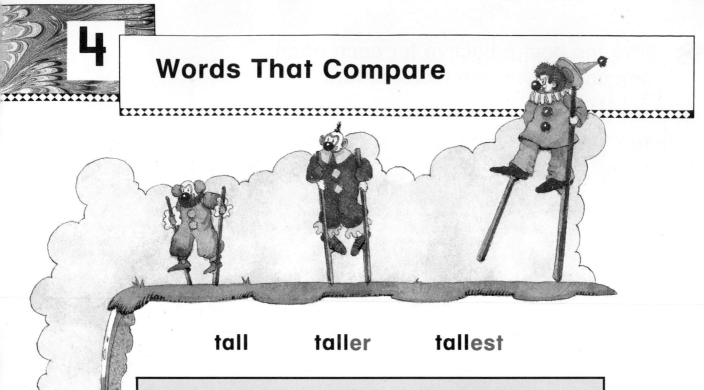

4 Words That Compare

tall   **tall**er   **tall**est

◆ Add **-er** to an adjective to compare two persons, places, or things.

◆ Add **-est** to an adjective to compare three or more persons, places, or things.

◆ Add **-er** and **-est** to the words below.

1. cold
3. soft
5. high

2. deep
4. long
6. old

◆ Add **-er** to the words in ( ).

7. The (small) ___ scooter is mine.

8. The sidewalk is (smooth) ___ on this block.

9. Our ride seems (short) ___ every time.

10. Today the sun feels (warm) ___.

◆ Add **-est** to the words in ( ).

11. The (old) ___ bike in the race won.

12. The (new) ___ bike came in second.

13. When you race, you want the (fast) ___ bike.

14. The winner often has the (straight) ___ path.

◆ Add **-er** or **-est** to the words in ( ).
Think first if two or more things are compared.

15. We walked our bikes up the (high) ___ hill of all.

16. We started from a (high) ___ spot than last time.

17. In this race the (slow) ___ racer of all wins.

18. It was a (slow) ___ walk going up again.

19. The (long) ___ walk of all was going home.

20. It felt like a (long) ___ road than before.

Apply Think about the best time you ever had outdoors.
Write about it. Use some adjectives that compare.

Using *a* and *an*

◆ Use **a** if a word begins with a consonant sound.

◆ Use **an** if a word begins with a vowel sound.

Write **a** or **an** for each sentence.

1. I tried to use ___ door that goes around.

2. It was ___ amazing door.

3. Finally ___ lady helped me get out.

4. She said ___ elevator is easier to use.

5. I pushed ___ button for the third floor.

6. There was ___ floor of stuffed animals.

7. Should I get ___ elephant?

8. My friend has ___ tiger.

9. Maybe he would like ___ anteater.

10. It is ___ unusual toy.

a door

an elevator

Apply   What is your favorite toy?
Write about why you like it.
Use **a** or **an** in your sentences.

use*ful*

use*less*

Suffix	Meaning	Example
-ful	full of	joy + ful = joyful
-less	without	rest + less = restless

◆ Write the word that has a suffix.

1. My sister is thoughtful.
2. She is so helpful.
3. Now my shoe is spotless.

4. It can be a thankless job.
5. I was useless when I did it.
6. Now I am more careful.

◆ Add **-ful** or **-less** to the word in ( ).

7. I was (hope) ___ jumping rope.

8. My friend was (cheer) ___ and taught me how.

9. Her pretty pictures are so (color) ___ .

10. I was (care) ___ and spilled the paint.

Writing with Adjectives

Adjectives tell more information about nouns. Adjectives can also make your writing more interesting. Which sentence sounds better to you?

A. I have a kitten.
B. I have a soft gray kitten.

Both sentences tell about a pet, but **B** tells what the kitten looks like and feels like. Other adjectives could tell that the kitten is **tiny** and **playful**. Adjectives add word pictures to your writing.

The Grammar Game ♦ These pairs of adjectives and nouns do not belong together. Write the adjective that makes sense for each noun.

fuzzy penny   foggy box   crunchy sky
shiny clown   happy carrot   square peach

1. ____ penny   **3.** ____ box   **5.** ____ sky
2. ____ clown   **4.** ____ carrot   **6.** ____ peach

Working Together

Your group can use adjectives to make your writing more interesting.

▸ Try a game of alphabet adjectives! Agree on adjectives to add to the sentences. The first one shows an example.

1. Susan sings a <u>silly</u> song.

2. Norman needs ___ news.

3. Harry hears ___ horns.

4. Bill buys a ___ book.

In Your Group

♦ Write down everyone's ideas.
♦ Help each other think of ideas.
♦ Let a speaker finish before you start.

♦ WORD FINDER ♦

Finish the rhyme with adjectives. Look up **big** in the Word Finder. Try to use **big** and each of the other words in the best place.

I heard the mayor say,
"Today's our town's <u>a</u> day!"
The <u>b</u> parade will be grand
With a <u>c</u> marching band,
And a <u>d</u> fireworks display!

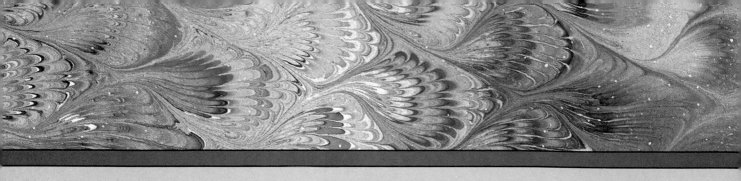

HOT ROD
painting by Norman Rockwell
printed by permission of the Estate of Norman Rockwell
copyright 1926 Estate of Norman Rockwell
Photograph courtesy Saturday Evening Post Marketing Company

UNIT FOUR

USING LANGUAGE TO
CREATE

=== PART TWO ===

Literature   Poetry

A Reason for Writing   Creating

CREATIVE
Writing

FINE ARTS ◆ Look at the painting at the left. Would you like to ride in that hot rod? The hot rod needs a bumper sticker. What should it say? Write your bumper sticker for the hot rod in the picture.

CRITICAL THINKING ♦
A Strategy for Creating

An Observation Chart

To observe means to notice. Notice these stars. What do you observe about them?

A pattern is something that is repeated over and over. What is the pattern of the stars?

◆ Sometimes you can see patterns. Look at this chart. Each row has a pattern. Copy the chart. Draw each pattern one more time.

Patterns I Can See
△ ▢ △ ▢ △ ▢
▲▲◼ ▲▲▲◼ ▲▲▲◼
♡ ◇ ◇ ♡ ◇ ◇
★ ◯ ♡ ★ ♡ ◯ ★ ◯ ♡

Sometimes you can hear patterns. Read aloud each row below. Do you hear a pattern? Say each pattern one more time.

Patterns I Can Hear
sun fun sun fun sun fun
where bear bear where bear bear
buzz buzz click buzz buzz click

You can make your own patterns. Think of two shapes or two sounds. Make up a pattern to draw or say. Show or tell it to a friend.

Next you will read some poems. Listen for words that repeat or rhyme. Listen for patterns in the poems.

Apply

♦ How did you figure out the patterns? How did you know what to draw or say next?

♦ Can you see or hear any patterns in your school? Where?

LITERATURE

Poets often write about their everyday lives.
Poets also like to imagine funny things that might happen.
In their poems they share what they think.
Sometimes it is something real. Sometimes it is
a silly thought. Did you
ever have ideas like these?

I Am Running in a Circle

I am running in a circle
and my feet are getting sore,
and my head is
spinning
spinning
as it's never spun before,
I am
dizzy
dizzy
dizzy.
Oh! I cannot bear much more,
I am trapped in a
revolving
. . . volving
. . . volving
. . . volving door!

— Jack Prelutsky

Berries on
the Bushes

Berries on the bushes
In the summer sun.
Bring along a bucket
And pluck every one.

Look at my teeth,
They're raspberry red.
Look at my fingers,
They're strawberry pink.
Look at my mouth,
It's huckleberry purple.
Look at my tongue,
It's blackberry ink.

— *Eve Merriam*

Unusual
Shoelaces

To lace my shoes
I use spaghetti.
Teacher and friends
All think I'm batty.

Let 'em laugh, the whole
Kit and kaboodle.
But I'll get by.
I use my noodle.

— *X.J. Kennedy*

I Woke Up One Morning

I woke up one morning
Without any head,
So I jumped to the floor.
And looked under the bed,
Then under my pillow,
The table,
The chair,
But look where I would,
My head wasn't there.
Not on the ceiling,
Not on the floor,
Not in the tree,
Not near the door.
Then at last I remembered—
Sure enough, just like that,
I found my old head!
It was under my hat.

— *Arnold Spilka*

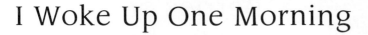

I Left My Head

I left my head
somewhere
today.
Put it down for
just
a minute.
Under the
table?
On a chair?
Wish I were
able
to say
where.
Everything I need
is
in it!

— *Lilian Moore*

 Reader's Response

Which poem do you think is the funniest? Tell why.

Poetry

 ## Responding to Literature

1. Music has rhythm. Many poems do, too. Listen as your teacher reads "I Am Running in a Circle." Keep the beat by clapping your hands or tapping your feet.

2. What do "Oh, you lost your head!" and "You really used your noodle." really mean?

3. Can you imagine having spaghetti shoelaces? Draw yourself in a silly poem.

 ## Writing to Learn

Think and Observe ♦ Look closely at an animal. What do you see? Write your ideas in a chart.

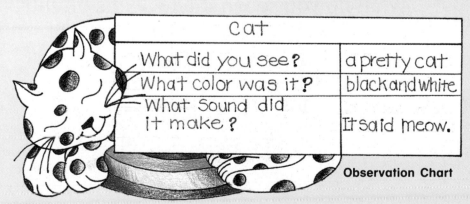

cat	
What did you see?	a pretty cat
What color was it?	black and white
What sound did it make?	It said meow.

Observation Chart

Write ♦ Use what you wrote in your chart. Write some sentences about your animal.

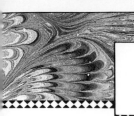

Rhyming two words is fun. It makes a sound pattern that we like to hear. Many poets use rhyming words in pairs.

A **rhyming couplet** is a pair of lines that rhyme. In a poem with rhyming couplets, the last words in each pair of lines rhyme.

▶ Read this poem aloud.
Listen for the rhyming couplets.
Then listen as a classmate reads the poem.

Up you go,
     Down you see,
Here's a turnip for you and me.
Here's a pitcher, we'll go to town.
Oh, what a pity! We've fallen down!
What do you see in the heavens bright?
I see the moon and the stars at night.
What do you see on the earth, so near?
I see a frog, and his voice I hear.
What is he saying there on the rock?
"Get up, get up! Warrah! Warrock!"

—*Chinese Mother Goose Rhyme*

◆ Write two pairs of rhyming words
from the poem.

◆ Write a list of words that rhyme with **bright**.

◆ Now think about what you see in the sky at night.
Write an answer to the poet's question.

"What do you see in the heavens bright?

_____ .

You may use a rhyming word from your list.

◆ Read this poem that has two rhyming couplets.
Write the pairs of rhyming words.

> Dilly dilly Piccalilli
> Tell me something very silly:
> There was a chap his name was Bert
> He ate the buttons off his shirt.
> —*Clyde Watson*

Apply Copy the beginning of the poem below.
Then think of something that is very silly.
It might be something you have seen or imagined.
Write a rhyming couplet to finish this poem.

> Dilly Dilly Piccalilli
> Tell me something very silly:
> There was a _____

_____ .

Now draw a picture to go with your poem.

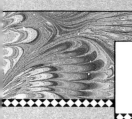

Some poems are easy to act out.

◆ Read this poem.

Rope Rhyme

Get set, ready now, jump right in
Bounce and kick and giggle and spin
Listen to the rope when it hits the ground
Listen to that clappedy-slappedy sound
Jump right up when it tells you to
Come back down, whatever you do
Count to a hundred, count by ten
Start to count all over again
That's what jumping is all about
Get set, ready now,
                          jump
                              right
                                  out!
—*Eloise Greenfield*

◆ Listen as your classmates read the poem aloud.
Write the words that make you want to move.

◆ Imagine that you have a jump rope in your hands.
Think about the words in the poem.
Move your arms as if you were jumping rope.

◆ Act out two lines from the poem.
See if your classmates can guess
which lines you are acting out.

◆ Draw a picture of yourself jumping rope.

Apply Pretend you are a jump rope.
Write how you feel when you are in the air.
Write what happens when you hit the ground.

Saying a Poem Together

Say this poem with your classmates.
Your teacher will divide the class into three groups.

Balloono

All: Balloono, Balloono,
    What do you bring
Flying from your fingers
    And fifty bits of string?

Group 1: Is it the sun
    Or is it the moon
Or is it a football
    For Saturday afternoon?

Group 2: A peach or a melon?
    Tell me, please.
An orange or an apple
    Or a big Dutch cheese?

Group 3: See them tugging
    In the bright blue air
As if they would wander
    Everywhere!

All: Come back, Balloono,
    When I draw my pay
And I'll buy them and fly them
    All away.

—*Charles Causley*

◆ What other things does a balloon remind you of?
Draw a picture of some of these things.

◆ Read this poem aloud with your classmates.

Catching-Song

All: You can't catch *me*!
You can't catch *me*!

Group 1: Run as swift as quicksilver,

All: You can't catch *me*!

Group 2: If you can catch me you shall
 have a ball
That once the daughter of a
 king let fall;

Group 3: It ran down the hill and it
 rolled on the plain,
And the king's daughter never
 caught her ball again,

All: And you can't catch *me*!
You can't catch *me*!

Group 1: Run as quick as lightning,

All: But you can't catch *me*!

—*Eleanor Farjeon*

◆ The poet says she will give you a ball if you
can catch her. Tell what gift you might give to
your friends if they caught you.

◆ **Apply** Find another poem in this book to
read aloud with your classmates. Choose groups
and decide which lines each group will say.

Writing a Poem

Sometimes a poem can be funny. Do you remember "I Am Running in a Circle"? It was about getting trapped in a revolving door. Do you remember "Unusual Shoelaces"? It was about tying shoes with spaghetti!

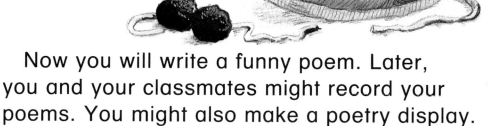

Now you will write a funny poem. Later, you and your classmates might record your poems. You might also make a poetry display.

1 Prewriting

Get ready to write. First choose a topic for your poem. Then get some ideas about it.

Choose Your Topic ◆ Think about something funny that you saw or did. It can be real or make-believe. Draw a picture of it. Write a sentence on the picture.

Show your picture to a partner. If your partner smiles, you have a good topic!

I put my boots on the wrong feet.

Choose Your Plan ◆ Here are two ways to get ideas about your topic. Choose the plan that is better for you.

PREWRITING IDEAS

Plan One ◆ Questions and Answers

Look at the picture you drew. Make up **Who, What**, and **Why** questions about it. Write your questions and answers. Your answers can be ideas for your poem.

Who did something funny?
I did.
What happened?
I walked funny.
Why did it happen?
I put my boots on the wrong feet.

Plan Two ◆ An Observation Chart

Imagine you could step into your picture. Make a chart. Write things you would see there. Write sounds you would hear. Your chart can give you ideas for your poem.

Inside My Picture	
What I see	boots feet rain puddles
What I hear	splashing in puddles boots going squish

2 Writing

How can you begin your poem? Get ideas from the poems in this book. Many begin with *I*. You might like to begin that way, too.

Get ideas from the picture you drew. Get ideas from the notes you wrote. Write lines about the funny thing that happened. Try to make your readers smile.

Would you like to have a pattern in your poem? You might use some words that rhyme. You might repeat some words.

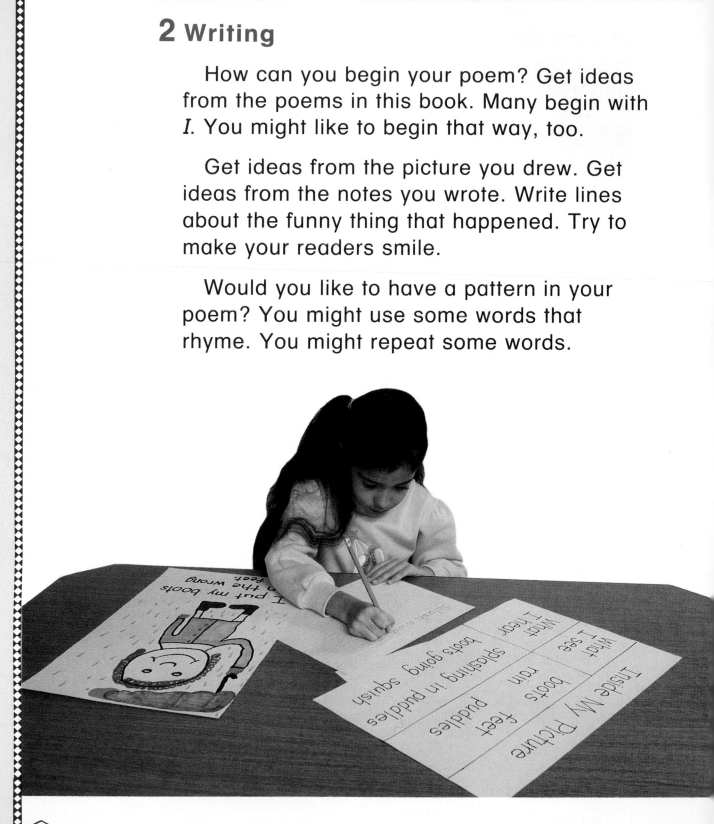

3 Revising

Read Rosa's poem. Can you see why she changed a word? Can you see why she added a word?

REVISING
MARKS

— cross
out

∧ add

Splash, squish.

My ~~toes~~ boots do not meet.

Splash, squish.

they∧ are on the rong feet!

REVISING IDEA

Read your poem aloud to yourself. Then read it to a partner. Do you like the way it sounds? Talk about how to make it better.

◆ Does my poem tell about something funny?

◆ Do I hear a pattern in my poem?

◆ Should I add any words or take any words out?

Grammar Check ◆ Did I use adjectives in my poem?

Now revise your poem. Make changes you think will make it better.

4 Proofreading

Look for mistakes you need to fix. These questions may help you.

♦ Did I spell each word correctly?

♦ Did I use capital letters correctly?

♦ Did I use the correct mark at the end of each sentence?

Now add a title. Then make a neat copy of your poem.

PROOFREADING MARKS

⬭ check spelling

☰ capital letter

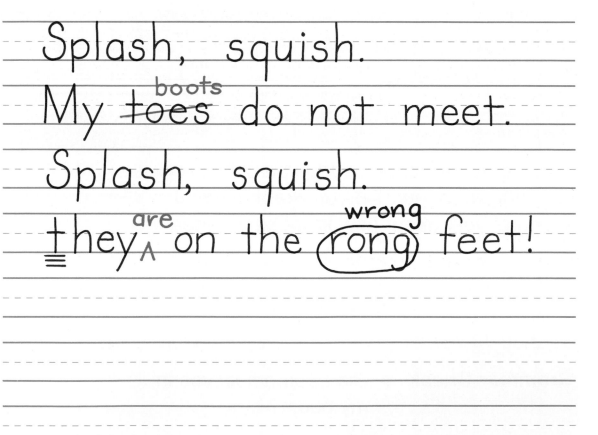

Splash, squish.

My ~~toes~~ boots do not meet.

Splash, squish.

they are on the ~~rong~~ wrong feet!

5 Publishing

Here are two ways to share your poem.

PUBLISHING IDEAS

Share Aloud

Read your poem into a tape recorder. Play the tape for your classmates. Ask them to tell what was funny about your poem.

Share in Writing

Display all your poems on a bulletin board. Read each poem. Write special words like **Wow, Good,** or **Nice!** Sign your name. Place your encouraging words on poems you liked.

Oops!
Splash, squish.
My boots do not meet.
Splash, squish.
They are on the wrong feet!

CURRICULUM
◆CONNECTION◆

Writing for Art

An artist takes things such as paint or clay and creates something wonderful. You are an artist, too. Sometimes you use crayons or paint. Sometimes you use words. Writing is an art. Writing can also help you learn about art.

"Paris Through a Window"
painting by Marc Chagall, 1913
Collection, Solomon R. Gugggenheim
Foundation, New York.

Writing to Learn

Think and Observe ◆ Look at this painting. Pretend you are in the picture. Make an observation chart.

Write ◆ Write what you would see and hear if you were in the picture.

Writing in Your Journal

Did you find a few funny ideas in this unit? Was there a picture that made you smile? Write about one of the ideas or pictures that made you laugh.

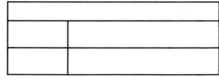

Observation Chart

Read More About It

More Surprises
by Lee Bennett Hopkins
No idea is too big or too small
for a poem. You will find many
surprises in this collection.

The Rooster Crows
by Maud and Miska Petersham
Many of these rhymes and games
may be familiar to you. Which ones
do you know? **Caldecott Medal**

Book Report Idea   Comic Strip

Make a comic strip for a book
you enjoy. Draw two or three
boxes. Draw some people in the
boxes. Show what they say
about your book. Write their
words in balloons near them.

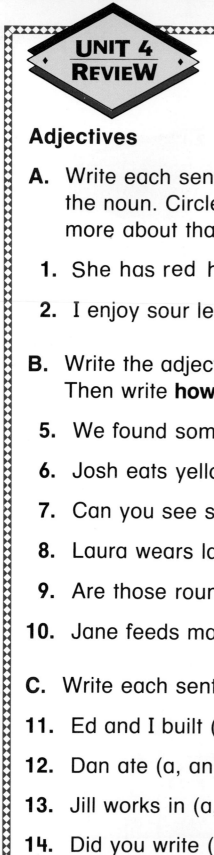

Adjectives

A. Write each sentence. Put a line under the noun. Circle the adjective that tells more about that noun.

1. She has red hair.

2. I enjoy sour lemons.

3. They played soft music.

4. You have two pens.

B. Write the adjective from each sentence. Then write **how many** or **what kind** for each one.

5. We found some paper.

6. Josh eats yellow apples.

7. Can you see six fish?

8. Laura wears large hats.

9. Are those round beads?

10. Jane feeds many pets.

C. Write each sentence. Use **a** or **an**.

11. Ed and I built (a, an) house.

12. Dan ate (a, an) orange.

13. Jill works in (a, an) office.

14. Did you write (a, an) story?

D. Decide if two or more things are being compared. Then add **-er** or **-est** to the adjectives in ( ). Write the sentences. Use the new adjectives.

15. Mary's skates look (new) ___ than before.

16. Sam has the (new) ___ skates of all.

17. My poem is (long) ___ than his.

18. Her poem is the (long) ___ of all.

Poems

E. Choose a word in ( ). Write the rhyme.

19. When he reached the top
He had to (run, stop).

20. All the drops of rain
Hit the window (pane, sill).

F. Write your own words to finish the poem below. Use a rhyming word at the end.

One red ball that rolls
Two green socks with holes
Three birds in a tree

_____ .

CUMULATIVE REVIEW

Sentences

A. Write the sentence in each pair.

1. a. Her pretty jacket
   b. Beth tore her jacket.

2. a. Throws the ball
   b. Ali throws the ball.

B. Write each statement or question correctly.

3. did your team win

4. she hit a home run

C. Write each sentence. Circle the naming part.
Put a line under the telling part.

5. We play softball.

6. Ken wears a glove.

7. Our friends came late.

8. Vicky caught the ball.

Nouns

D. Write the noun in each sentence.

9. The field is wet.

10. We went to the game.

11. That girl plays often.

12. They waved to the team.

E. Write the nouns that mean more than one.

13. man   men

14. cup   cups

15. dish   dishes

16. mice   mouse

17. feet   foot

18. box   boxes

F. Write the nouns that show ownership.

    19. my brother's lunch   **20.** the doctor's office

Verbs

G. Write each sentence. Use the correct verb in ( ).

    21. Cars (move, moves) fast.

    22. Lora (bake, bakes) bread.

    23. The child (sit, sits) there.

    24. Trees (grow, grows) slowly.

H. Add **-ed** to the verb in ( ). Write the new verb.

    25. The team (watch) the clock.

    26. The band (play) our song.

    27. Val and Mary (jump) up.

    28. We (cheer) loudly.

Adjectives

I. Write the adjective in each sentence. Then write **how many** or **what kind** for each one.

    29. Steve found six rocks.

    30. They were grey rocks.

    31. Dena picked many flowers.

    32. They saw colorful shells.

LAZY RIVER CAMPGROUND

EASILY REACHED FROM MANY ROADS, WE HAVE PLENTY OF WATER,
HAY, AND SHADE TREES. THIS IS A FAVORITE STOPPING PLACE
FOR TRAVELING CIRCUSES. THIS IS A FAVORITE STOPPING PLACE
REWARDED BY THE SIGHT OF A CIRCUS ON ITS WAY AT DAWN.

Dear Ma, Pa and Grandpa,
    We stayed in the exact same
campground as the circus
    We got here in the
and me w
in the

funny shoe. I think
it's a <u>lucky</u> shoe.
Potato loves this
shoe!

INTERNATIONAL
SOMERSAULT
GAMES
U.S.A.

W

Illustration by Vera B. Williams
and Jennifer Williams

USING LANGUAGE
TO
INFORM

==== **PART ONE** ====

Unit Theme   *Sending Messages*

Language Awareness   Nouns and Pronouns

==== **PART TWO** ====

Literature   *Stringbean's Trip to the Shining Sea*
by Vera B. Williams and Jennifer Williams

A Reason for Writing   Informing

Writing
IN YOUR JOURNAL

WRITER'S WARM-UP ◆ Stringbean wrote some postcards to his family. Writing is only one way to send a message. You might wink, move your head or arm, or make a sound. Write in your journal about one way you would like to send someone a message. Tell how you would send it.

Names and Titles for People

Note on message board:

Pam —
Please pack for our trip.
Take your address book.
Help jenny pack too.
Remind grandma to feed rusty.

Dad —
Call ed kane in texas

Mom —
At 5 o'clock sue ryan called

♦ The names of people, pets, and places begin with capital letters.

◆ The names in the message center should begin with capital letters. Write the names correctly in the sentences.

1. Pam has to help ___ pack.

2. She has to tell ___ to feed ___.

3. Dad should call his friend ___.

4. Dad's friend lives in ___.

5. Mom received a call from ___.

♦ Titles for people begin with capital letters.
  Most titles end with a period.

 6–11. Write this story carefully.
Remember to write titles correctly.

In the post office, miss Ellen Judge sorts
the mail. Later, the postal worker will deliver
it to ms Sally Hope, mr Harry Logan, mrs Joan
Maris, miss Fay Chen, and dr Thomas Carp.

Apply Write your teacher's name and title correctly.

Titles of Books

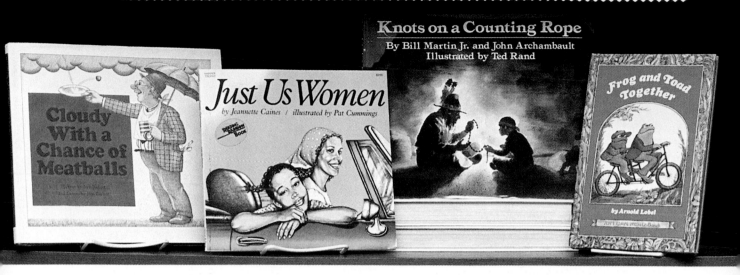

♦ Begin the first, last and all important words in a book title with capital letters. Draw a line under the title.

◆ Write these book titles correctly.

1. little bear

2. millions of cats

3. ira sleeps over

4. a letter to amy

5. green eggs and ham

6. alice in wonderland

7. a bargain for frances

8. the little red hen

Apply Pretend you are the author of a new book. What would it be about? Write the title of your book correctly.

3 Days of the Week

♦ The names of the days of the week begin with capital letters.

Read Todd's calendar pages.
Then write each sentence with the correct day.

1. Todd visits the museum on ___ .

2. On ___ and ___ he uses a secret code.

3. He writes to his pen pal on ___ .

4. On ___ Todd goes to see a play.

5. His music lesson is on ___ .

6. Todd visits the lighthouse on ___ .

Apply What is your favorite day? Write a sentence about it.

Months, Holidays, and Special Days

> ◆ The names of months, holidays, and special days begin with capital letters.

1–6. Write each month in Cathy's story correctly.

Last year was a busy one. In july and august we drove to the ocean. I wrote to a pen pal in march, and in april I got a letter back. She will visit next june. My friends and I visited a nursing home in october. The people came to our play after our visit.

◆ Now write the holidays and special days in Cathy's story correctly.

Last year I marched in three parades. They were on memorial day, columbus day, and thanksgiving. Our class went outside to look for a shadow on groundhog day.

For halloween I was a computer. Then we used computers to make cards for mother's day and father's day. We had a ceremony for our new flag on flag day.

5 Pronouns

Captain Rand and Ms. Norris send messages.
They send messages.

The word **they** is a pronoun.
It takes the place of the words **Captain Rand and Ms. Norris.**

> ◆ A **pronoun** takes the place of a noun.

◆ The words **he, she, it, we, you,** and **they** are pronouns.
Write the sentences.
Circle the pronouns in the sentences.

1. When Columbus sailed, he could not use lighthouses.
2. In 1492, they were not yet invented.
3. Today we know most ships need signals.
4. Ms. Norris says she will be moving soon.
5. In a while you will not find people in lighthouses.
6. Then they will just have machines to make signals.
7. Did you ever visit a lighthouse?
8. Last summer we did.
9. Beautiful stone was used to build it.

◆ Match the names in ( ) with the pronouns.

10. (Ms. Norris) is a lighthouse keeper.   **a.** They
11. (Mr. Rand) is a captain.   **b.** She
12. (Mr. and Mrs. Lu) are teachers.   **c.** We
13. (Dr. Wood and I) play tennis.   **d.** He

◆ Write pronouns for the words in ( ).
Use **He, She, It, They,** and **We.**

14. (Sara and I) went on the main deck.
    ___ saw a sailor working.

15. (The sailor) put flags on a rope.
    ___ said each flag stands for a letter.

16. (The flags) are used to send a message.
    ___ can be seen from other ships.

17. (The message) has the letters **C** and **N**.
    ___ uses one flag for each letter.

18. (Sara) saw another ship nearby.
    ___ saw flags on that ship, too.

Apply Pretend you found a message in a bottle.
What might it say? Use pronouns in your message.

6 Using *I* and *me*

**Liz, Al, and I went to the ocean.
Al found a card for me.**

I is used in the naming part of a sentence.
The pronoun **me** is used in the telling part.

♦ Always write **I** with a capital letter.

♦ Always name yourself last.

Write I or me for each sentence.

1. My family and ___ went to the ocean last summer.
2. My sister made a sand castle for ___ .
3. Liz and ___ looked for shells.
4. She carried some shells for ___ .
5. My friends and ___ like to get postcards.
6. Al and ___ mailed some to our friends.
7. Someone may mail a card to ___ .

Apply Think of a postcard message you might write
to a friend. Use **I** and **me** in your message.

VOCABULARY ♦
Words That Sound Alike

I can hear the ocean in here.

> ♦ Some words sound alike but have different meanings and spellings.

◢ Find two words that sound alike in each pair of sentences. Then write them.

1. The ship is out at sea.
   I can see a long way.

2. Write your letter.
   Mail it right away.

3. I saw their book.
   It is over there.

4. Will you meet me?
   Do you like meat?

5. A soft wind blew.
   The blue kite fell.

6. Who ate an apple?
   There were eight of them.

Write a sentence using **two** and **too.**

VOCABULARY: Homophones **175**

Writing with Pronouns

You have been using pronouns to replace nouns. You can use a pronoun instead of repeating the same noun too many times. Which sentence below sounds better?

A. Nancy wrote a letter and mailed the letter.

B. Nancy wrote a letter and mailed it.

Both sentences tell the same thing about Nancy, but in sentence **A** the words **the letter** are repeated. Sentence **B** sounds better. What pronoun is used instead of the words **the letter**?

The Grammar Game ◆ Unscramble the pronouns! Write them. Next to each pronoun, write the nouns from the list that each pronoun can replace.

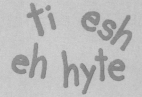

Mr. Ramos	butterfly
Anita	Jan and Dean
trucks	Mrs. O'Connor

Working Together

Use pronouns in your group instead of repeating nouns too many times.

◆ Finish these lines from songs. Agree on the pronouns to use. Write each pronoun.

In Your Group

- ◆ Make sure everyone has a turn.
- ◆ Help others remember the group's ideas.
- ◆ Use quiet voices when you talk.

1. Twinkle, twinkle little star,
   How ___ wonder what ___ are.

2. Six little ducks that ___ once knew

3. This old man, ___ played one

◆ WORD FINDER ◆

Solve these riddles. Look up **building** in the Word Finder. Write the name of a building instead of the word **it** in each riddle.

a. **It** is full of books to borrow.
b. **It** is where one family lives.
c. **It** holds many students and teachers.
d. **It** is a place where many families live.

PHILLIS WHEATLEY
copperplate engraving, Anonymous, 1773
Culver Pictures, Inc.

USING LANGUAGE
TO
INFORM

=== **PART TWO** ===

Literature *Stringbean's Trip to the Shining Sea*
by Vera B. Williams and Jennifer Williams

A Reason for Writing Informing

CREATIVE
Writing

FINE ARTS ◆ The picture at the left shows Phillis Wheatley. She was a famous writer. Will you be famous some day? Will you be an astronaut? An athlete? A doctor? Draw a picture of yourself as someone famous. Write your name and why you are famous.

A Strategy for Informing

A Prediction Chart

Predicting is guessing what will happen. Read this story about Rita. Then predict what she might do next.

Rita likes to draw. She draws animals. Rita went hiking in the woods. She took lunch, crayons, and drawing paper with her. Rita hiked for a long time. Then she saw a deer. The deer was taking a drink from a pond.

◆ What do you predict Rita will do next? Look for clues in the story. Then draw a picture. Show what you predict Rita will do.

◆ Find the end of the story at the bottom of this page. Then copy and complete this prediction chart.

My Prediction	What Happened
I predicted that Rita would ___ .	What Rita did was ___ .

Rita took out her paper and crayons. She drew a picture of the deer.

Was your prediction right? Was it fun to guess? Was it fun to find out?

Next you will read about a boy named Stringbean. Stringbean goes camping with his brother and his dog. They drive west by truck. Stringbean writes postcards about what he sees on the trip.

◆ What will Stringbean see on his trip? Draw one thing you predict he might see.

◆ Copy the prediction chart below. Complete the first box now. After you read about Stringbean, complete the second box.

My Prediction	What Happened
I predict that Stringbean will see ___ .	What Stringbean did see was ___ .

Apply

♦ How did you predict what Stringbean might see?

♦ Do you ever try to predict what will happen? Why?

LITERATURE

from

Vera B. Williams

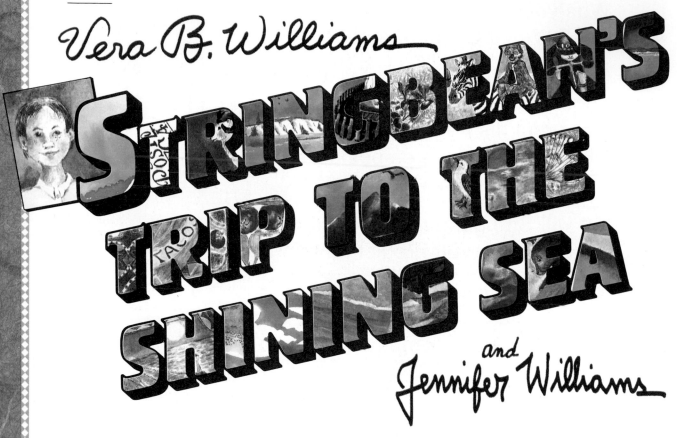

STRINGBEAN'S TRIP TO THE SHINING SEA

and Jennifer Williams

One summer Stringbean Coe and his older brother Fred took a long trip. They drove west by truck to the Pacific Ocean. Stringbean's dog Potato went along, but Fred's rabbit Lily stayed home.

Every day Stringbean sent a postcard home to his family back in Kansas. He told all about their adventures. Here are two postcards that Stringbean wrote.

INTERNATIONAL
SOMERSAULT
GAMES
U.S.A.

W

funny shoe. I think
it's a lucky shoe.
Potato loves this
shoe! love Stringbean

LAZY RIVER CAMPGROUND
EASILY REACHED FROM MANY ROADS, WE HAVE PLENTY OF WATER, HAY, AND SHADE TREES. THIS IS A FAVORITE STOPPING PLACE FOR TRAVELING CIRCUSES. EARLY-RISING CAMPERS ARE OFTEN REWARDED BY THE SIGHT OF A CIRCUS ON ITS WAY AT DAWN.

Dear Ma, Pa and Grandpa,
We stayed in the exact same
campground as the circus!!☆**✦
We got here in the dark. Potato
and me were asleep already. But
in the morning I was looking out
at a big old elephant. [really].
But we only got to see them pack-
ing up and moving out with their
trucks and all their thur stuff. It
was so early there were still stars
up in the sky.
   After when I was looking around
I found one of the clowns great.
big shoes! I hope they have extras.
Freddy says we'll catch up to them
so we can give it back. It's a big

ARTIST: JENNIFER WILLIAMS

PUT YOUR BUSINESS ON A CARD

□ □ □ THIS SPACE FOR ADDRESS

COE FAMILY
COE SPRINGS MOTEL
JELOWAY, KS.
66708

P.S. We are going to stay at
a Buffalo Ranch tomorrow
tonight. I am excited.
This isn't such good printing
because I did it too fast.

AMERICAN BISON, or BUFFALO
Before hunting made them extinct in the wild, buffalo roamed the plains of the U.S. and Canada by the millions. Cow or Buffalo Birds flew around them and slept in the wool of their manes at night.

Dear Ma, 🌸 🌸 🌸

Remember I cried that time you told me too much hunting had killed off almost every buffalo. NOW THERE ARE BUFFALO AGAIN.

One reason is Mr. Harlee Hawkins. He started this ranch with just 4 wild buffalo. Now there are 200. He is a Sioux. His grandma told him how once buffalo used to cross the river for 6 days and 6 nights. And there were so many passenger pigeons it made the sky dark. There were so many eagles. There were so many elk. 🌸... 🌸.... 🌸 ...

Mr. Hawkins says the exact same thing grandpa says, "Well kid that was then. This is now."

I love the way buffalos have curls growing down their noses. Ask aunt Tina for me, "Would you like if a buffalo came to your beauty parlor for a shampoo?"

love and hugs × × × × × ×

ARTIST: JENNIFER WILLIAMS
NATURE CARDS SERIES #1—ANIMALS

Dear Folks,
I hope Lily is doing well. I'm wishing for a big litter.

🐇 🐇 🐇
Love Fred

THE COE
FAMILY
COE SPRINGS MOTEL

JELOWAY, KS.

66708

P.S.
So far no trouble with truck.
Stringbean checks the oil and tires
so don't worry.
F.
× × Stringbean ♡

Library Link ✦ *You can read all the rest of Stringbean's postcards in the book* Stringbean's Trip to the Shining Sea.

 ## Reader's Response

Would you like to travel with Stringbean and Fred? Tell why.

LITERATURE: Story

Stringbean's Trip to the Shining Sea

 ## Responding to Literature

1. Would you like to read more postcards from Stringbean? Tell why.

2. Write a postcard to a friend. Tell about an interesting thing that happened to you recently.

3. How do you think Stringbean got his name? Write your idea. Draw a picture of what you think Stringbean looks like.

 ## Writing to Learn

Think and Predict ◆ You know that Stringbean found a clown's shoe. What do you predict will happen to the shoe? Fill in a chart to tell what you know about the shoe.

What I Know About the Shoe	What I Predict Will Happen to the Shoe
Stringbean found it. Potato likes it. It belongs to a clown. It is really big.	

Prediction Chart

Write ◆ Write what you predict will happen to the shoe.

Glen received this invitation. It tells

- ♦ who is invited
- ♦ what the event is
- ♦ when to come
- ♦ where to come
- ♦ who sent the invitation

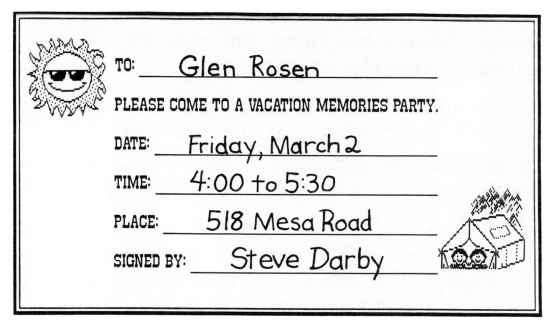

TO: __Glen Rosen__

PLEASE COME TO A VACATION MEMORIES PARTY.

DATE: __Friday, March 2__

TIME: __4:00 to 5:30__

PLACE: __518 Mesa Road__

SIGNED BY: __Steve Darby__

◆ Use the invitation to complete each sentence.

1. Glen is invited to a ___ .

2. The party is on ___ .

3. It is from ___ o'clock until ___ .

4. The party is at ___ .

5. The invitation is from ___ .

◆ Copy the invitation. Use these parts.

| King's Roller Palace   Sue   Skating Party |

Make up your own date and time.
Sign your name.

To: ___

Please come to a ___.

Date: ___

Time: ___ to ___

Place: ___.

Signed by: ___

◆ Look at your invitation.
Did you fill in all of the information?
Do the date and the time make sense?

Apply Make an invitation for a special
party. Draw a design that goes with the
party on the border of your paper.
Then write the important information.

Read this friendly letter from Stringbean. Notice the five parts: the **date, greeting, body, closing,** and **signature.**

Each **comma** ⟨,⟩ is in blue. A comma is used between the date and year. Commas are also used after the greeting and closing. The first word of the greeting and closing begins with a capital letter.

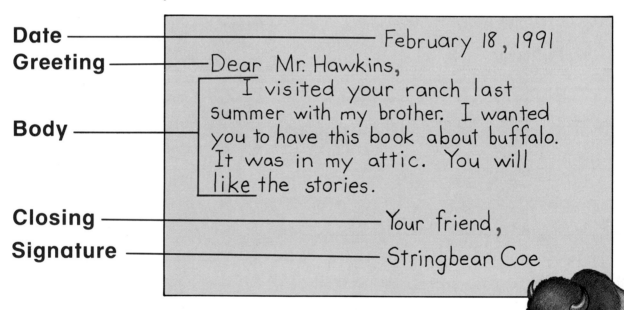

Date ——————————————————————— February 18, 1991
Greeting ——————— Dear Mr. Hawkins,

Body ———————
    I visited your ranch last summer with my brother. I wanted you to have this book about buffalo. It was in my attic. You will like the stories.

Closing ——————————————————————— Your friend,
Signature ——————————————————— Stringbean Coe

◆ Write the answers to these questions.

1. Who is the letter to?
2. Which part tells the message?
3. What is the closing?
4. How many commas did Stringbean use?

◆ Write a friendly letter to Stringbean.
Tell him about one of these:

- ◆ your family
- ◆ your school
- ◆ where you live
- ◆ an adventure you had

Make sure your letter has five parts.
Put commas and capital letters where
they belong.

◆ Write a friendly letter to a pen pal.
Tell the pen pal about yourself.

Apply Pretend you are someone famous.
Write a letter to a partner. Give hints
about yourself. Do not sign your name.
Have your partner guess who you are.

Writing a Thank-You Letter

A thank-you letter has the same parts as a friendly letter. The body thanks someone for something.

◆ Read this thank-you letter about a class trip.

March 3, 1991

Dear Miss Russo,
    Thank you for letting us visit you. Your darkroom was the best part. We liked seeing how photographs become postcards.

Your friends,
Ms. Mann's class

◆ Write a thank-you letter to the author of your favorite book. Tell about the part you liked best.

An envelope has two addresses. The
return address tells who is sending
the letter. The **mailing address** tells
who will receive the letter. Use a
comma [,] between the city and the state.

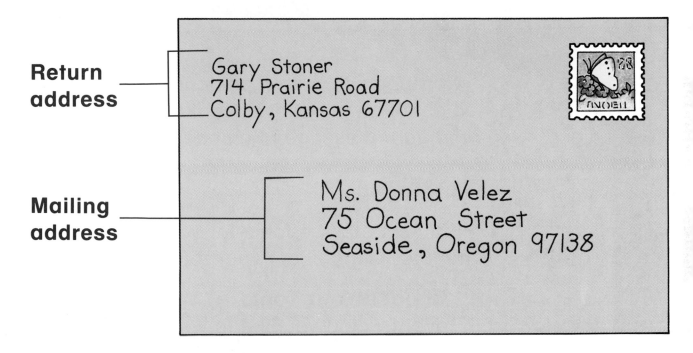

**Return
address**

Gary Stoner
714 Prairie Road
Colby, Kansas 67701

**Mailing
address**

Ms. Donna Velez
75 Ocean Street
Seaside, Oregon 97138

◆ Write the answers to these questions.

1. Who will receive the letter?

2. Who is sending the letter?

Apply Make an envelope. Address it to
Stringbean Coe. Use your own return address.

Writing a Postcard

You read part of *Stringbean's Trip to the Shining Sea*. Stringbean's postcards tell the story of his adventure.

Now you will write a postcard. You will tell about an event or adventure. You will write your message to a special person.

1 Prewriting

First choose the topic for your message. Then get ideas about your topic.

Choose Your Topic ◆ What adventure or event would you like to write about? You might write about a trip like Stringbean's. You could write about doing something for the first time. Did you visit a farm and milk a cow? Perhaps you ran in a race.

Make your postcard on five-by-eight-inch cardboard. On the front, draw a picture about your special event. On the back, make spaces for the message, address, and stamp.

Choose Your Plan ◆ Here are two plans for getting ideas about your topic. Choose the one you think will help you more.

PREWRITING IDEAS

Plan One ◆ Talking

Work with a partner. Look at the picture you drew on your postcard. Talk about the event. Who was there? What happened? What did you see or hear? How did you feel? Were you excited? Were you scared? Did you laugh a lot? Tell your partner all about it.

Plan Two ◆ A Prediction Chart

Look at the picture you drew on your postcard. Think about the event. What did you predict would happen before the event? What really happened? Was it what you predicted? Were there any surprises? Write your answers in a prediction chart.

My Prediction	What Happened
I thought I would be too scared to run in the race.	I was scared, but I ran anyway. I came in second!

2 Writing

You learned about the parts of a friendly letter. A postcard message is shorter. It only needs a greeting, a body, and a signature.

Write your message on a piece of paper first. Begin with a friendly greeting. You might write **Dear Yoko,** or **Hi, Grandpa**. Say hello any way you wish.

Now start to write your message. Look at your drawing. Think about what you told your partner. Did you make a prediction chart? These things can give you ideas.

Remember that the message space is small. Who will get your card? What will that person most want to know? Write a short message. Then sign your name.

3 Revising

Here is Jesse's postcard message. He added the greeting and a sentence and changed a word.

REVISING MARKS

— cross out

∧ add

Hi, Grandpa!

My teacher mr. Green asked me to run a race. ∧ I _I came in second._ was skared, but I ran. I wish ~~Grandpa~~ you had seen me.

Jesse

REVISING IDEA

Read your message to yourself, then to a partner. Talk about how to make it better.

◆ Did I write a greeting and a signature?

◆ Does my message tell about an event?

Grammar Check ◆ Did I use titles correctly?

Now revise to make your message better.

4 Proofreading

Look for mistakes you need to fix. Ask yourself these questions.

◆ Did I spell each word correctly?

◆ Did I use capital letters correctly?

◆ Did I use the correct mark at the end of each sentence?

Now copy your message neatly onto your postcard.

PROOFREADING MARKS	
⬭	check spelling
≡	capital letter

Hi, Grandpa!

My teacher mr. Green
                    ≡   I came in second.
asked me to run a race. ᴧ I

         scared
was (skared) but I ran. I

              you
wish G̶r̶a̶n̶d̶p̶a̶ had seen me.

                    Jesse

5 Publishing

Here are two ways to share your postcard.

PUBLISHING IDEAS

Share Aloud

Take part in a class "Adventure Day." Show your postcard to your classmates. Read your message aloud. Let classmates tell if they have had adventures like yours.

message

Hi, Grandpa!
My teacher
Mr. Green asked
me to run a race.
I was scared,
but I ran. I
came in second.
I wish you had
seen me.
      Jesse

stamp

address

Mr. Frank Washington
13 Peachtree Way
Atlanta, GA 30305

Share in Writing

You may wish to send your postcard. Then you will need to address it. Use the address of the person you wrote to. Write it next to your message. Maybe your special person will write back!

Writing for Music

People love music. Sometimes people dance to music. Sometimes they sing. Some people even send messages with music. You can predict what music will do.

Writing to Learn

Think and Predict ◆ Musicians love to play for other people. What do you think will happen when the musicians in this picture play? Think about it. Then make a prediction chart.

Write ◆ Write what you know about the picture. Then write what you think will happen next.

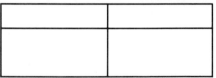

Prediction Chart

Writing in Your Journal

Music is one way to send a message. Writing a postcard is another. Write about an interesting way you would like to send someone a message.

BOOKS TO ENJOY

Read More About It

Three Days on a River in a Red Canoe
by Vera B. Williams
A family goes camping and canoeing. The author of this book also wrote the book about Stringbean.

A Letter to Amy *by Ezra Jack Keats*
The wind carries away Amy's invitation to Peter's party. How will Amy know about the party?

Book Report Idea   Book Stamp

Design a stamp for one of your favorite books. Cut some paper in a stamp shape. Write the name of the book along one edge. Draw a picture to go with the story.

Nouns

A. Write each name or title correctly.

1. ms ann long

4. i met a man

2. february

5. virginia

3. mr mark cole

6. saturday

Pronouns

B. Write the sentences. Use **He**, **She**, **It**, and **We** for the words in (   ).

7. (Carol) works.

9. (Scott) is home.

8. (Pat and I) jump.

10. (The book) is open.

C. Write **I** in each sentence correctly.

11. Joan and i go skating.

12. Now i will read this book.

D. Write each sentence. Use **I** or **me** correctly.

13. Soon (I, me) will visit Eric.

14. Peg drove Sue and (I, me).

15. Sal and (I, me) play ball.

16. Don sits next to (I, me).

Letters

E. Write a friendly letter. Use these parts.

Your friend,	Dear Charlie,

March 3, 1991	David

> I liked visiting you.
>
> Your new game was so much fun.

F. Write these parts of the friendly letter. Then write **date**, **greeting**, **closing**, and **signature** next to the correct parts.

17. David
18. Your friend,
19. March 3, 1991
20. Dear Charlie,

UNIT SIX

USING LANGUAGE TO
NARRATE

=== PART ONE ===

Unit Theme   *Remembering My Past*

Language Awareness   Verbs

=== PART TWO ===

Literature   *The Josefina Story Quilt* **by Eleanor Coerr**

A Reason for Writing   Narrating

Writing
IN YOUR JOURNAL

WRITER'S WARM-UP ◆ When we remember something special, we can enjoy it again and again. Do you remember your first day at school? Do you remember the first time you rode a bike? Write in your journal. Write about something you remember.

1

Using *is* and *are*

Alex is happy today.   **That stamp is red.**
He and Grandpa are busy. **Those pages are full.**

Now	One	is
	More than one	are

◆ Read the sentences and the chart above.
Then write **is** or **are** for each sentence.

1. Alex ___ proud of his stamps.

2. His new book ___ from Grandpa.

3. Those stamps ___ the oldest.

4. Grandpa and Alex ___ careful.

5. Two blue stamps ___ ready.

6. This one ___ Alex's favorite.

7. Three big flags ___ on it.

8. The biggest stamp ___ there.

9. It ___ on the first page.

10. This hobby ___ lots of fun.

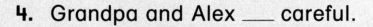

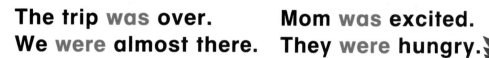

2 Using *was* and *were*

The trip was over.   **Mom was excited.**
We were almost there. **They were hungry.**

In the Past	One	was
	More than one	were

◆ Read the sentences and the chart above. Then write **was** or **were** for the story.

Our visit __a__ last Saturday. My new kitten __b__ in the car. We __c__ a little tired because the ride __d__ long. Grandmother __e__ at the gate. My cousins __f__ there, too. I __g__ so glad! My family and I __h__ ready for lunch.

3

Using *has* and *have*

Grandmother has a farm.   **It has an old barn.**
She and I have a good visit.   **We have fun there.**

Now	One	has
	More than one	have

▶ Read the sentences and the chart above.
Then write **has** or **have** for the story.

My grandmother __a__ an old farmhouse.

It __b__ large bedrooms. Some beds __c__

pretty quilts. The quilts __d__ many colors.

They __e__ some squares from old

dresses. Two of them __f__ big stars in

the corners. That one __g__ a log cabin.

Each quilt __h__ its own story.

4 Using *come* and *run*

We come to the lake often.   **Jan runs into the water.**
Last night they came here.   **Last year I ran in first.**

Now	come, comes	run, runs
In the Past	came	ran

Read the sentences and the chart above.
Then write the correct word from each ( ) below.

1. For years we (come, came) to this lake.

2. Now we always (come, came) with the Lin family.

3. Yesterday my dog (runs, ran) after a frog.

4. He jumps up and (runs, ran) to me now.

5. We swim and (run, ran) with him.

6. Now the water (comes, came) up to my knees.

7. Years ago it (comes, came) up to my chin.

5 Using *give* and *take*

Today I give Meg a picture.   **Now Dad takes some.**
Last night they gave me one.   **Then the boys took turns.**

Now	give, gives	take, takes
In the Past	gave	took

◆ Read the sentences and the chart above.
Write the correct word from each ( ) below.

1. Dad (gives, gave) me a scrapbook
   last year.

2. He (gives, gave) me help with it now.

3. Now we (take, took) more pictures.

4. Last fall Mr. Santos (takes, took) a

   picture of our soccer team.

5. After that he (gives, gave) me a copy.

6. Meg comes and (takes, took) a look.

7. Now I always (give, gave) copies to her.

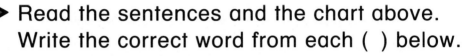

Using *do* and *go*

Today I do my job.   **Now he goes in a car.**
Last night she did hers.   **Then they went by wagon.**

Now	do, does	go, goes
In the Past	did	went

◆ Read the sentences and the chart above.
Then write the correct word from each ( ) below.

1. Years ago some people (do, did) something new.

2. They left their homes and (go, went) West.

3. Now many people (go, went) by airplane.

4. Long ago families (go, went) slowly in wagons.

5. Today they (do, did) the trip
   in a few hours.

6. Yesterday I (do, did) a
   report for school.

7. Now Ed (does, did) a drawing
   of covered wagons.

8. I think it (goes, went) well
   with my report now.

This quilt is not finished.
This quilt isn't finished.

The word **isn't** is a contraction.
It is a short way of writing **is** and **not**.
An apostrophe ⟨ ' ⟩ takes the place of **o** in **not**.

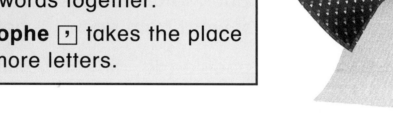

- ◆ A **contraction** is a short way
  to put two words together.
- ◆ An **apostrophe** ⟨ ' ⟩ takes the place
  of one or more letters.

◆ Write the contraction for each pair of words.

1. is not	**a.** don't	**6.** has not	**f.** shouldn't
2. are not	**b.** didn't	**7.** have not	**g.** couldn't
3. do not	**c.** isn't	**8.** could not	**h.** hasn't
4. does not	**d.** aren't	**9.** would not	**i.** haven't
5. did not	**e.** doesn't	**10.** should not	**j.** wouldn't

◆ Write the contractions for the words in ( ).

11. Alice (did not) ___ sew her square yet.

12. She (could not) ___ find a needle.

13. I (have not) ___ done mine either.

We will make a class quilt.
We'll make a class quilt.

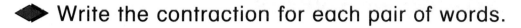

The word **we'll** is a contraction for **we will**.
An apostrophe takes the place of **wi** in **will**.

 Write the contraction for each pair of words.

14.	I will	**k.**	she'll	**19.**	I am	**p.**	we're
15.	he will	**l.**	they'll	**20.**	he is	**q.**	she's
16.	she will	**m.**	I'll	**21.**	she is	**r.**	they're
17.	we will	**n.**	he'll	**22.**	we are	**s.**	he's
18.	they will	**o.**	we'll	**23.**	they are	**t.**	I'm

Write the contractions for the words in ( ).

24. (We are) ____ using paper and glue.

25. (He is) ____ painting his square.

26. Soon (you will) ____ see our quilt on the wall.

Apply What would you put on a quilt square?
Write a sentence about it. Use a contraction.

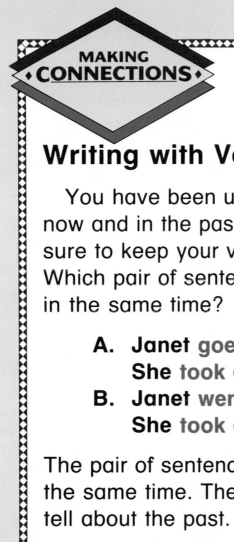

MAKING ◆CONNECTIONS◆

Writing with Verbs

You have been using verbs to tell about now and in the past. When you write, be sure to keep your verbs in the same time. Which pair of sentences has both verbs in the same time?

**A. Janet goes to see a friend.
She took a present.**

**B. Janet went to see a friend.
She took a present.**

The pair of sentences in **B** have verbs in the same time. The verbs **went** and **took** tell about the past.

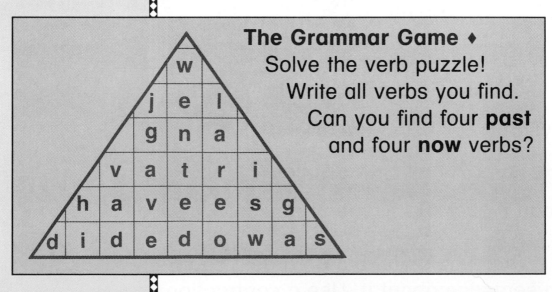

The Grammar Game ◆
Solve the verb puzzle!
Write all verbs you find.
Can you find four **past**
and four **now** verbs?

Working Together

Keep verbs in the same time.

◆ Agree on words to complete the paragraph. Make all the verbs tell about the past. Write the paragraph.

Bob's best friend **is** here. When summer **comes**, they often **go** to the library. They **take** out books about the olden days.

In Your Group

♦ Help others understand what to do.
♦ Help each other think of ideas.
♦ Help the group finish on time.

◆ WORD FINDER ◆

Look up **say** in the Word Finder. Use **say** and three of the other words to finish the rhyme.

How do you say what you say?
   What's the rule?
When teachers __a__ your name at school,
Do you __b__ your answer in a nice clear way?
Or do you __c__ very loudly as if far away?
Do you __d__ so people can hardly hear you?
How do you say it? What do you do?

THE QUILTING PARTY
oil and pencil on paper, adhered to plywood; Anonymous, c. 1860
Abby Aldridge Folk Art Center, Williamsburg, Virginia.

USING LANGUAGE
TO
NARRATE

═══ **PART TWO** ═══

Literature   *The Josefina Story Quilt* by Eleanor Coerr

A Reason for Writing   Narrating

CREATIVE
Writing

FINE ARTS ◆ Would you like to be at the party in the picture at the left. What do you like to do at parties? Write about your favorite kind of party. Tell why you like to go to parties.

A Strategy for Narrating

A Prediction Chart

Predicting is guessing what will happen. Read this story. Predict what will happen.

It was 1845. The Miller family were going west in a covered wagon. Their cousins were in another wagon. It was almost dark. They wanted to reach the wagon camp. Suddenly, a wheel broke!

◆ What do you predict the Millers will do? Copy this chart. Complete the first box.

My Prediction	What Happened
What will the Millers do? I predict the Millers will ____ .	What did the Millers do? What the Millers did was ____ .

◆ How did you figure out your prediction? Did common sense help? Were there any clues in the story? Find the end of the story at the bottom of this page. Then complete the second box of the chart.

The Millers rode to camp with their cousins. They fixed their wagon the next day.

Next you will read *The Josefina Story Quilt.* It is about Faith and her family. They are going west in a covered wagon.

It will be a long trip. Faith wants to remember it. How can she remember the trip? How can she make a record of what happens?

◆ Look at the pictures that go with the story. Think about the story title. How do you predict Faith will record her journey?

◆ Copy the prediction chart below. Complete the first box now. Then read *The Josefina Story Quilt.* Afterwards, complete the second box of the chart.

My Prediction	What Happened
How will Faith record her journey? I predict that Faith will ___ .	How did Faith record her journey? What Faith did was ___ .

◆ How did you figure out your prediction for Faith?

◆ Can predictions always be right? Why or why not?

LITERATURE

from

The Josefina Story Quilt

By Eleanor Coerr   Pictures by Bruce Degen

*It was May 1850. Faith and her family were moving
to California. It would be a great adventure.
They would go across the country in a big covered wagon.
Many families would travel together in a long wagon train.*

*Everything a family needed to live in a new place
had to fit in their wagon.
Some things would have to be left behind.
Would there be enough room for Faith's pet hen, Josefina?*

California, Ho!

Early in the morning
the wagon was ready.
It had blue trim and
a white cloth roof.
Ma stood back to admire it.
"A big flowerpot on wheels!" she said.
"Isn't it beautiful?"
Faith did not answer.
She was worried about Josefina.
"Did you pack the food?" Ma asked Pa.
"And my kitchen things?" Pa nodded.
"Then that is everything
except the bedding," said Ma.
Faith thought sadly, "And Josefina."

Pa threw mattresses into the wagon. Ma carefully spread their patchwork quilts over them. "We can't leave these behind," she said. "All our joys and sorrows are sewn up into the patches."

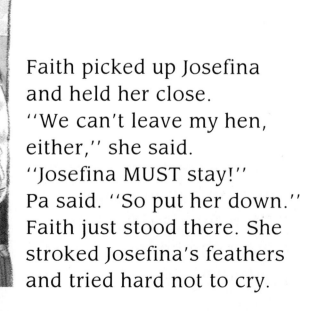

Faith picked up Josefina and held her close. "We can't leave my hen, either," she said. "Josefina MUST stay!" Pa said. "So put her down." Faith just stood there. She stroked Josefina's feathers and tried hard not to cry.

LITERATURE: Story

Ma gave Pa a special look. Pa sighed. "All right, Faith," he said. "But if she makes any trouble, OUT SHE GOES!"
"Thank you, Pa!" cried Faith.
"She will be good, I promise."

Faith put Josefina in her cage. Pa hung it high up at the back of the wagon. Then he lifted Faith up next to it. Ma handed her the ragbag. "Work on a patch whenever you can," she said. Faith knew how important quilts were for remembering.

"California, ho!" shouted Pa.
He snapped his long whip.
C R A A A A C K!
The oxen began to move.
Their bells tinkled.
The heavy wagon chains clanked.
And the wheels began their creaky song.

Faith smiled happily at Josefina. This would be their home on the long trail West. Faith took some calico from the ragbag. "I will make my first wagon train patch," she said. Faith began to sew a wagon wheel with careful, tiny stitches.

The trip in the wagon was long and hard. There were many dangers. Josefina turned out to be a big help with some of the family's problems along the way. Finally the wagon train reached California. The family built a new home. Then Pa made a quilting frame. The whole family helped Faith stitch her patches together.

The new quilt was finished. The patches helped Faith always remember the journey in the covered wagon.

Library Link ◆ *You can read more about Faith's adventures in the book* The Josefina Story Quilt *by Eleanor Coerr.*

 Reader's Response

Do you think a quilt can be like a journal? Tell how.

LITERATURE: Story

The Josefina Story Quilt

Responding to Literature

1. If you moved, what would you most want to take with you? Choose only one thing.

2. With a few classmates, plan a Readers Theatre for *The Josefina Story Quilt*. You need one reader for the narrator and one for each character.

3. Make a square for a class quilt. Draw something you especially want to remember about this year in school.

Writing to Learn

Think and Predict ♦ Copy this chart. Add other things you know about this quilt.

What I Know About Faith's Quilt	What I Predict Will Happen to the Quilt
She made it herself. It took a long time to make. Her mother made quilts too.	

Prediction Chart

Write ♦ Write what you predict will happen to Faith's quilt.

Finding the Main Idea

Faith's family was moving to California. It would be an adventure. They would cross the country in a big covered wagon. Many families would travel together in a long wagon train.

The sentences above are all about one idea. That idea is called the **main idea**. The main idea is that Faith's family was going to California. Read the sentence that tells the main idea.

◆ Read the sentences below.
Write the sentence that tells the main idea.

1.   Every family had its own wagon. They packed everything they needed for the journey in the wagon. Only a few things were left behind.

   ♦ They packed everything they needed for the journey in the wagon.

   ♦ Every family had its own wagon.

   ♦ Only a few things were left behind.

Read each group of sentences below. Write the main idea.

2. A covered wagon was large. It had to carry people and their things. The wheels were as tall as a child. The cloth roof was like a great tent.

3. The wagon started to move. The oxen pounded a rhythm on the hard ground. The wheels groaned as they turned.

4. Every day there was something new to see. John was amazed when he saw a herd of deer. Their antlers were huge! The next day he saw mountains for the first time.

5. Life on the trail was not always easy. Sometimes the people were too cold. Sometimes they did not have enough food or water.

Apply Turn back to the story. Read page 223. Tell the main idea in your own words.

Finding Details

When you write, you use details to give information. A **detail** tells more about the main idea. There may be more than one detail in a group of sentences.

◆ Read the group of sentences below. The blue sentence tells the main idea. It says that Faith had a pet hen. The green sentences give details about the main idea. They tell more about the hen.

> Faith had a pet hen. Her name was Josefina. Faith wanted to bring Josefina on the trip to California.

◆ **1–2.** Read this group of sentences about Faith's family. The blue sentence tells the main idea. Write the details that tell about the main idea.

> The family prepared to leave on their journey. Pa gathered the tools he would need. Ma put the pots and pans in the wagon.

3. Read this group of sentences about the wagon. Write the main idea.

> The wagon was their home on the long trail West. Faith and her parents slept inside. The wagon protected them when it rained. It held all of their belongings.

4–6. Now write three details that tell about the main idea. Use your own words.

Apply Read the sentence below the picture. It tells a main idea.

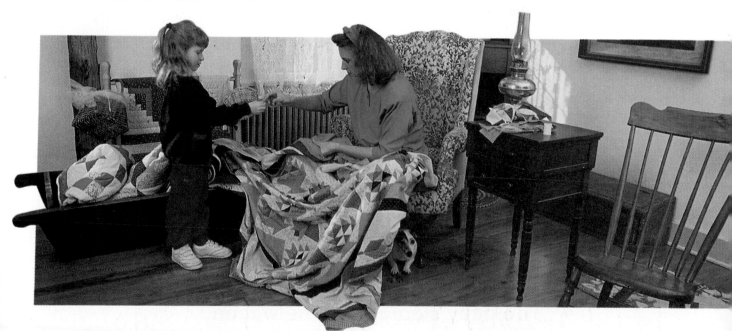

A handmade quilt is special.

Now look at pages 220 to 224.
Find details that tell more about this main idea.
Tell the details in your own words.

Writing a Main Idea and Details

Read this sentence. It tells a main idea.

It was hard to drive a covered wagon.

Read these details. Some tell more about the main idea. Some do not tell about the main idea.

> ◆ Ma yelled to the oxen to keep moving.
> ◆ They cooked food over an open fire.
> ◆ The baby slept inside the wagon.
> ◆ When a wheel broke, Pa fixed it.

◆ Find the details that tell more about the main idea. Write the main idea. Then write the details.

Read these main idea sentences.
Each one tells about the picture.

- ♦ The quilt patch is made of many shapes.
- ♦ The pieces fit together like a puzzle.
- ♦ The house sits in a field of snow. .

Which main idea do you like best?
Write the sentence. Then write details
that tell more about the sentence.

Apply What event do you like to remember? Write a
sentence that tells a main idea about it. Draw a
picture to show details about your main idea.

WRITING PROCESS
NARRATING

Writing a Story

The Josefina Story Quilt told the story of Faith's journey. You learned how she went to California. You learned what she did and how she felt.

Now you will write a true story. It will be about a journey you have taken. Later you can share your story on a make-believe TV show or in a story display.

1 Prewriting

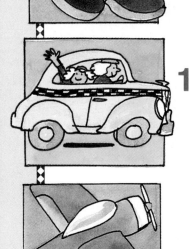

Get ready to write. First choose your topic. Then get ideas about your topic.

Choose Your Topic ♦ A journey can be long or short, near or far. What journeys have you taken? Did you visit a new place on vacation? Did you go to your grandmother's house? Your story may be about a walk to the library. It may be about a hike in the park.

Faith rode in a covered wagon. How did you travel? Did you walk, ride, or fly? Did you travel a different way? Draw the way you traveled on a piece of paper.

Choose Your Plan ♦ Here are two plans for getting ideas. Choose one to try.

Plan One ♦ A Picture

Draw a picture of yourself. Show yourself on your journey. Ask yourself these questions. Write answers on your picture.

♦ Where are you going?
♦ Who is traveling with you?
♦ What one special thing happened?
♦ How did you feel?

I went to Ames Park with Mom.
We saw a waterfall.
We hiked.
I felt peaceful.

Plan Two ♦ A Prediction Chart

What did you predict would happen on your journey? What really did happen? Was it what you predicted? Were there any surprises? Write your answers in a prediction chart.

My Prediction	What Happened
I thought my feet would hurt. I thought I would not like hiking.	My feet hurt a little, but it was very peaceful. I had a good time with Mom.

2 Writing

Before you write, look at your picture or your chart. Then begin your story. Start with a sentence that tells the main idea. Read these beginnings for ideas.

♦ I will always remember my trip to . . . .

♦ The last time I visited Grandma . . . .

♦ The first time I went hiking . . . .

As you write, tell where you went. Tell who went with you. Tell what happened. Did things happen that you predicted? Did something happen that you didn't expect? How did you feel?

Use your prewriting notes to help you recall details. Make sure all the details tell about your main idea.

3 Revising

Jesse wrote and revised this story. He added details that told how he felt.

REVISING MARKS

— cross out

∧ add

mom and I ~~go~~ ^went^ hiking in Ames Park. We walked and walked ^a lot^. I thot my feet would hurt. ^They hurt just a little.^ We saw birds ^and fish^ and a waterfall. ^I felt peaceful and happy with my mom.^

REVISING IDEA

Read your story to yourself. Then read it to a partner. Talk about how to improve it.

◆ Did I tell the main idea, where I went?

◆ Did I tell how I felt?

Grammar Check ◆ Did I use the correct verbs for one and more than one?

Now revise to make your story better.

4 Proofreading

Do you need to fix any mistakes? These questions may help you find them.

♦ Did I spell each word correctly?

♦ Did I use capital letters correctly?

♦ Did I use the correct mark at the end of each sentence?

Now add a title. Then make a neat copy of your story.

mom and I ~~go~~ went hiking in Ames Park. We walked and walked. I ~~thot~~ thought my feet would hurt. They hurt just a little. We saw birds and fish and a waterfall. I felt peaceful and happy with my mom.

5 Publishing

Here are two ways you might share your story.

PUBLISHING IDEAS

Share Aloud

Have a classroom TV show. Cut a television screen from a cardboard box. Face the class through the screen and read your story. Ask your viewers to phone in questions about your journey. You can answer on the air.

Our Family Hike
Mom and I went hiking in Ames Park. We walked and walked. I thought my feet would hurt a lot. They hurt just a little. We saw birds and fish and a waterfall. I felt peaceful and happy with my mom.

Share in Writing

Make a travel poster for your school cafeteria. Hang your story on poster paper. Add pictures that show your journey. Put some sheets of paper with your display. Invite readers' comments.

CURRICULUM
·CONNECTION·

 ## Writing for Mathematics

In math you sometimes find patterns of shapes or numbers. You need to decide what shape or number comes next. You can use writing to help you decide.

Writing to Learn

Think and Predict ◆ Look at the shapes below. What shape comes first? Second? Third? When does the pattern begin again? Make a prediction chart.

  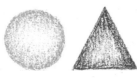

Write ◆ Write what you know about the pattern. Write the three shapes that come next. Use the words **circle, square,** and **triangle.**

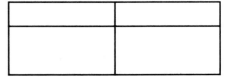

Prediction Chart

 ## Writing in Your Journal

In this unit you have read about different ways people save their memories. Write about one way you like to remember someone or something.

BOOKS TO ENJOY

 ## Read More About It

The Quilt Story *by Tony Johnston*
Abigail loves her quilt, but she
must pack it away. Years pass,
and another girl finds the quilt.
What does the new owner think?

Emma *by Wendy Kesselman*
Do you like to paint or draw?
Read about Emma's special
way of remembering her past.

 ## Book Report Idea   Paper Fold

Fold long paper into four parts.
On the first part write the title
and author of a book you like.
Write a sentence about the
beginning of the book on the
next part of your paper. Use
the last two parts to tell about
the middle and the end of
your book. You may draw
some pictures, too.

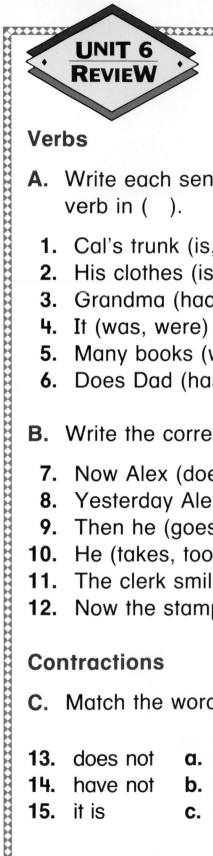

UNIT 6 REVIEW

Verbs

A. Write each sentence. Use the correct verb in ( ).

1. Cal's trunk (is, are) here.
2. His clothes (is, are) in it.
3. Grandma (had, have) a trunk.
4. It (was, were) in the hall.
5. Many books (was, were) in it.
6. Does Dad (has, have) a trunk?

B. Write the correct verb in ( ).

7. Now Alex (does, did) like to collect stamps.
8. Yesterday Alex (runs, ran) to thank Grandpa.
9. Then he (goes, went) to buy more stamps.
10. He (takes, took) his album with him last week.
11. The clerk smiles and (gives, gave) Alex his change.
12. Now the stamps (come, came) in a flat case.

Contractions

C. Match the words with their contractions.

13. does not	**a.** haven't		16. they will	**d.** we're
14. have not	**b.** it's		17. I am	**e.** they'll
15. it is	**c.** doesn't		18. we are	**f.** I'm

Main Idea and Details

D. Read each group of sentences. Write the sentence that tells the main idea.

19. Everyone picked vegetables. I helped Mom can them. Then we put them away for winter.

20. People made clothing from wool. Sheep's wool was used. Vegetables gave it color.

21. Aunt Nora made a quilt for me. I put it on my bed. It was nice and fluffy.

22. Ben received a camera. He bought film. Then Dad helped him take pictures.

E. Read the group of sentences below. Then follow the directions.

We went to a festival. There were many displays. We watched people make candles and corncob dolls. Some bees made honey.

23. Write the sentence that tells the main idea.

24–26. Write the details that tell about the main idea.

Illustration by John Schoenherr

UNIT SEVEN

USING LANGUAGE TO DESCRIBE

═══════════════ **PART ONE** ═══════════════

Unit Theme *Weather*

Language Awareness Adverbs

═══════════════ **PART TWO** ═══════════════

Literature *Owl Moon* by Jane Yolen

A Reason for Writing Describing

IN YOUR JOURNAL

WRITER'S WARM-UP ◆ Weather brings us windy days and rain and snow. Weather also brings us warm, sunny days. What kind of weather do you like best? Why? Write about it in your journal.

Words That Tell *When* and *Where*

A cool wind blew today.
I went outside.

An adverb can tell **when** or **where**.
The word **today** tells **when** the wind blew.
The word **outside** tells **where** I went.

◆ An **adverb** tells more about a verb.

Copy the sentences below.
Draw a line under each verb.
Circle each adverb that tells when or where.

1. The rain started early.

2. Big drops came down.

3. My hat fell off.

4. The water splashed up.

5. I saw my cat there.

6. Patches ran inside.

7. Cats never like rain.

8. I often enjoy it!

Write the adverbs.
Write **when** if the adverb tells when.
Write **where** if the adverb tells where.

9. I go inside with my cat.

10. Patches shakes water everywhere.

11. Now the rain stops.

12. The clouds blow across.

13. Then the sky brightens.

14. The sun peeks out.

15. I put my umbrella away.

16. I forgot it yesterday.

17. Mom always remembers.

Apply   What do you like to do when it rains?
Write two sentences about you and the rain.
Use adverbs that tell when and where.
Circle the adverbs.

Words That Tell *How*

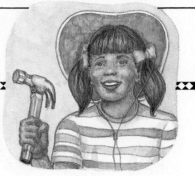

I held the hammer tightly.

An adverb can tell **how**.
Many adverbs that tell how end in **-ly**.
The word **tightly** tells how I held the hammer.

◆ Copy the sentences below.
Circle the adverbs that tell how.

1. We worked carefully.

2. Dad firmly held the wire.

3. I helped eagerly.

4. Mom spoke quietly.

5. Bob slowly carried the water.

6. I drank some thankfully.

7. The time passed quickly.

8. We finished the job gladly.

◆ Choose the adverb in ( ) that tells how.
Write each sentence.

9. The sun shines (often, here, brightly).

10. Dry winds blow (lightly, across, soon).

11. Desert flowers grow (now, slowly, inside).

12. My pony runs (swiftly, away, today).

13. It stops (outside, then, quietly).

14. Two rabbits sleep (never, silently, there).

15. A bird calls (loudly, always, down).

16. It flies (gracefully, early, up).

Apply Write this sentence.
Change the word in dark type to an adverb.

The feather landed **soft**.

Antonyms

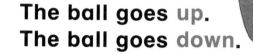

The ball goes up.
The ball goes down.

The words **up** and **down** are antonyms.
They have opposite meanings.

> ◆ **Antonyms** are words that have opposite meanings.

◆ Write the antonyms.

1.	noisy	**a.** start	**4.**	dry	**d.** outside
2.	win	**b.** quiet	**5.**	inside	**e.** push
3.	stop	**c.** lose	**6.**	pull	**f.** wet

◆ Find the antonyms for the words in ( ).
Then write them in the sentences.

7. Jan loves to play (outside).

8. The waves are (quiet).

9. My toes are (wet).

10. We (pull) the raft.

Find the antonyms for the words in dark type.
Write them in the sentences.

easy	night	under	big	short
lost	empty	high	stay	light

11. Each **day** the fog comes in.

12. It is **low** tide.

13. Those are **little** shells.

14. Are they **hard** to find?

15. A crab goes **over** the sand.

16. These rocks are **heavy**.

17. I **found** my shovel.

18. Is your bucket **full** yet?

19. We stay out a **long** time.

20. I don't want to **leave**.

 Write an antonym for each word below.

slow	small	open

Now share your work with a friend.
Did you write the same antonyms?

Writing with Adverbs

You know that adverbs tell more about verbs. Adverbs also make your writing more interesting. Which sentence tells more?

A. The sun was shining.

B. Yesterday the sun was shining brightly here.

Sentence **B** is much more interesting. **Yesterday**, **brightly**, and **here** are adverbs that tell you how, when, and where the sun was shining!

The Grammar Game ♦ Act out adverbs! Read each direction. Then add an adverb to tell more. Take turns acting out directions with a partner. Can you guess each other's actions?

1. Open the door ___ .

2. Feed the birds ___ .

3. Pour the water ___ .

4. Pull the weeds ___ .

Working Together

Use adverbs in your group to make your writing more interesting.

◆ How does your group work together? Agree on an adverb to add to each sentence. Try to use adverbs that tell **how**, **when**, and **where**. Write your sentences.

1. We talk ___ .
2. We agree ___ .
3. We work ___ .
4. We listen ___ .

In Your Group

♦ Make sure everyone shares ideas.
♦ Thank people for sharing ideas.
♦ Agree or disagree in a nice way.

♦ WORD FINDER ♦

Look up **well** in the Word Finder. Use **well** and each of the other words to complete the memory test below. Write each word that your group thinks of. Try the test yourself! How did you do?

How __a__ do you remember details? Think __b__ before you answer! Can you recall your best friend's birthday __c__ ? If you can, you pay attention __d__ !

A SUDDEN SHOWER AT OHASHI
Japanese print by Ando Hiroshige
The Metropolitan Museum of Art,
Purchase, 1918, Joseph Pulitzer Bequest.

UNIT SEVEN

USING LANGUAGE TO

DESCRIBE

PART TWO

Literature ***Owl Moon*** **by Jane Yolen**

A Reason for Writing Describing

CREATIVE *Writing*

FINE ARTS ◆ Look at the picture at the left. Will these people tell their families about the rain? What will they say? Write about the worst rainstorm you can remember. Tell what happened and where you were.

A Strategy for Describing

An Observation Chart

To observe means to notice. Do you have a pencil? Pick it up. Look at it. Feel it. What details do you notice about it?

You can make an observation chart. You can write details that you notice. Here is an observation chart about a pencil.

A Pencil			
What I see	long	yellow	black point
What I feel	sharp point		soft eraser

♦ Find an object in your desk or your pocket. Look at it carefully. Feel it. Then copy and complete this observation chart.

Name of Your Object	
What I see	
What I feel	

Would you like to observe your school? You can do it without even moving! Look around. What can you see from where you are sitting? Close your eyes and listen. What can you hear in your classroom? What can you hear from outside your classroom?

Now copy and complete this observation chart.

My School	
What I see	
What I hear	

Have you ever been outdoors at night? What did you observe? Did you hear anything? Did you feel anything? What did you see?

Next you will read the story *Owl Moon*. Find out what the author observed outdoors at night.

Apply

♦ What happens when you observe? How do you do it?

♦ Do you ever observe things? When?

CALDECOTT
MEDAL
1988

from OWL
MOON

by Jane Yolen
illustrated by John Schoenherr

On a cold dark winter night, a little girl is going owling with her father. She has waited to share this adventure for a long time. They crunch quietly over the snow, in search of the Great Horned Owl. She is full of silent hope. ''My brothers all said sometimes there's an owl and sometimes there isn't.''

We walked on.
I could feel the cold,
as if someone's icy hand
was palm-down on my back.
And my nose
and the tops of my cheeks
felt cold and hot
at the same time.
But I never said a word.
If you go owling
you have to be quiet
and make your own heat.

We went into the woods.
The shadows
were the blackest things
I had ever seen.
They stained the white snow.
My mouth felt furry,
for the scarf over it
was wet and warm.
I didn't ask
what kinds of things
hide behind black trees
in the middle of the night.
When you go owling
you have to be brave.

Then we came to a clearing in the dark woods. The moon was high above us. It seemed to fit exactly over the center of the clearing and the snow below it was whiter than the milk in a cereal bowl.

I sighed and Pa held up his hand at the sound.
I put my mittens
over the scarf
over my mouth
and listened hard.
And then Pa called:
"Whoo-whoo-who-who-who-whooooooo.
Whoo-whoo-who-who-who-whoooooooo."
I listened
and looked so hard
my ears hurt
and my eyes got cloudy
with the cold.
Pa raised his face
to call out again,
but before he could
open his mouth
an echo
came threading its way
through the trees.
"Whoo-whoo-who-who-who-whooooooo."

Library Link ♦ *You might enjoy reading the book* Owl Moon *by Jane Yolen to find out what happens on this owling adventure.*

 Reader's Response

Does this book make you want to go owling?
Tell why.

OWL MOON

Responding to Literature

1. In *Owl Moon*, it was important to look and listen carefully. Which sense do you think is more valuable? Tell why.

2. What sounds do you hear at night that you do not notice during the daytime?

3. The family in *Owl Moon* likes to go owling. What do you like to do with your family?

Writing to Learn

Think and Observe ◆ Spend some time outdoors. Fill in details on a chart like this one about what you see, hear, and feel.

Going Owling with My Dad	
What I saw	the moon, black trees, shadows, white snow
What I heard	Dad calling "whoo-whoo-who," myself breathing, our footsteps
How I felt	hot and cold at the same time, my ears hurt, cold all over

Observation Chart

Write ◆ Write a description about what you observed. Let your reader know exactly how you felt, and what you saw and heard.

What Is a Paragraph?

A **paragraph** is a group of sentences about one main idea. One sentence tells the main idea. The other sentences add details that tell more about it.

Read this paragraph.

Owls are great hunters. They have very good eyesight. They can move quickly and quietly. Owls can hold things in their strong claws as they fly.

Did you notice that the first word in the paragraph is **indented**? That means it is moved in a little to the right. The other sentences are not indented. They do not start on a new line.

◆ **1.** Write the sentence that tells the main idea.

◆ Read this paragraph.

Owls use their ears for hunting. They hear very tiny sounds. Owls hear sounds that our ears do not notice. That is how they catch mice in total darkness.

2. Write the sentence that tells the main idea.

3. Write a sentence that gives a detail about the main idea.

When you write a paragraph, the sentences must be in order. This helps the paragraph make sense.

Read these sentences. They are not in paragraph order.

Then she held out her arm. First she put on a long leather glove. The zoo worker showed us an owl. Last the owl rested on her arm.

4. Write the sentence that should come first in the paragraph.

5. Write the sentence that should come last in the paragraph.

Apply Write the sentences below as a paragraph. Put the sentences in an order that makes sense.

Most screech owls are only ten inches long.
The holes are small, too.
Screech owls are small birds.
They often live in holes in trees.

The main idea is the **topic** of a paragraph. Every sentence in a paragraph should keep to the topic.

◆ Read the paragraph about the night woods. One sentence does not keep to the topic. Write it.

> The woods were very still. Nothing was moving. That day was my birthday. Animals were hiding or sleeping. Even the moon was hidden.

Apply Write the paragraph. Leave out the sentence that does not keep to the topic. Remember to indent the first word.

> My shadow changes as light moves. Sometimes it is big and long. I am brave in the dark. At other times my shadow becomes shorter.

WRITING ◆
Telling Enough

When you write a paragraph, be sure you tell enough. Write enough details to answer your reader's questions. Ask yourself, "Is there anything else my reader would like to know?"

◆ Read this paragraph. It does not tell enough. What else do you want to know?

> It is a wonderful season. The air is nice. It is pretty. You can do things in this season.

◆ Write the paragraph. Add details to make the paragraph tell enough. Use your own words. The questions will help you tell more.

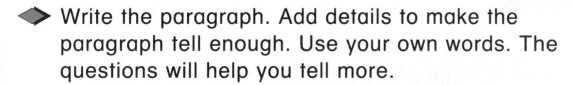

_____Which season?_____ is a wonderful season.

The air is _____What kind?_____ and _____What kind?_____ .

It is pretty _____What makes it pretty in that season?_____ .

You can _____What can you do?_____ in the _____What season?_____ .

Writing Descriptive Details

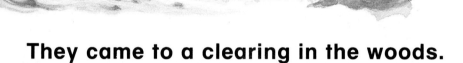

They came to a clearing in the woods.

Lee and his dad are walking in the woods. Pretend you are with them. Think about how things look, sound, feel, smell, and taste. Use your senses.

◆ The sentence below the picture tells the main idea. Now write details about the clearing in the woods.

1. Write a sentence telling how something looks.

2. Write a sentence telling how something sounds.

3. Write a sentence telling how something feels.

4. Write a sentence telling how something smells.

5. Write a sentence telling how something tastes.

Read the paragraph below.

>   We walked in the tall pine woods. The
> branches were white with snow. Our boots
> crunched as we walked. The snow felt like
> powder. The pine smell made us think of a
> campfire. The air tasted crisp.

The first sentence in the paragraph tells the main idea. It is about a walk in the pine woods. The other sentences describe the walk. These sentences tell how things look, sound, feel, smell, and taste. They give **descriptive details.**

6. Look at the picture. Write a sentence that tells the main idea.

7–8. Write two descriptive details that tell more about the main idea.

Apply Take turns playing a guessing game with a partner. Describe something that both of you have seen. Give one hint at a time. Tell how the object looks, sounds, feels, smells, or tastes.

WRITING PROCESS
DESCRIBING

Writing a Description

In *Owl Moon*, a girl describes the weather. She uses words like **icy, cold, snow**, and **wet**. Her description helps us feel we are there. Did you almost feel the cold?

Now you will write a paragraph. You will tell about the weather on a special day. Then you can read your description to your classmates. You may also make a mobile to share your writing.

1 Prewriting

Get ready to write. First choose your topic. Then get ideas about your topic.

Choose Your Topic ♦ Look at the word boxes below. Which kind of weather would you like to write about? Choose a box. Now you have your topic.

A Hot Day	A Wet Day	A Cold Day
hot	cloudy	cold
sun	wet	icy
burning	shivering	snow
thirsty	splashing	freezing

Choose Your Plan ◆ Here are two plans for getting ideas about your topic. Choose the plan you like better.

PREWRITING IDEAS

Plan One ◆ Colors

Draw a picture of yourself. Show yourself in the weather you chose. Then color the picture. Make it look hot, or wet, or cold.

Does your picture show you on a hot day? Use reds, oranges, and yellows. Is it a wet day? Use grays, silvers, and browns. Is your day cold? Try blue, violet, and white.

Show your picture to a partner. Talk about the kind of weather it shows.

Plan Two ◆ An Observation Chart

Think about the day you chose to describe. Close your eyes. Pretend you are outdoors on that day. Ask yourself these questions: "What do I see?" "What do I hear?" and "What do I feel?" Write your answers in an observation chart.

A Wet Day	
What I see	dark clouds large raindrops
What I Hear	rain drops pattering
What I feel	shivery wet

2 Writing

Before you write, look at your picture or chart. How will you begin your paragraph? Mention your topic, the weather, in the first sentence. Here are some ways to begin.

♦ The day was dark and cloudy.

♦ The winter day was cold and snowy.

♦ It was a hot and sunny day.

Now add details about your topic. Describe the weather and the day. Tell what you saw and what you heard. Tell what or how you felt. Did you taste or smell anything?

Remember, you are writing a description, not a story. Make your readers see what you saw. Help them hear, feel, taste, and smell what you did. Be sure every detail and sentence is about your topic.

WRITING PROCESS: Descriptive Paragraph

3 Revising

Jesse revised his paragraph. One sentence did not tell about a rainy day. He crossed it out. He added other details.

It was a rainy day. the clouds
were gray ∧and dark. Big drops were
∧pattering ~~falling~~ on the sidewak. I
~~love riding my bike.~~ My shirt
got ∧soaking wet. Then I ∧my skin felt was shivery.

REVISING IDEA

Read your paragraph to yourself. Then read it to a partner. Talk about ways to make it better.

◆ Do all the details tell about the topic?

◆ Did I tell my topic at the beginning?

Grammar Check ◆ Did I tell when, where and how things happened?

Now revise your paragraph. Make changes that you think will make it better.

4 Proofreading

Look for mistakes you should fix. These questions may help you find them.

◆ Did I indent the first word?

◆ Did I spell each word correctly?

◆ Did I use capital letters correctly?

◆ Did I use the correct mark at the end of each sentence?

Now make a neat copy of your paragraph.

PROOFREADING MARKS	
¶	indent
◯	check spelling
≡	capital letter

¶It was a rainy day. the clouds
were gray. _and dark_ Big drops were
pattering falling on the (sidewak). _sidewalk_ I
love riding my bike. My shirt
got wet. _soaking_ Then I was shivery. _my skin felt_

5 Publishing

Here are two ways you can share your paragraph.

Share Aloud

Sit with a small group of classmates. Take turns reading your paragraphs aloud to each other. Ask your listeners to name a detail they especially liked.

> A Wet Day
>
> It was a rainy day. The clouds were gray and dark. Big drops were pattering on the sidewalk. My shirt got soaking wet. Then my skin felt shivery.

Share in Writing

Put your paragraph and your picture or chart on cards. With a friend, make a mobile from the cards. Hang the mobile from the classroom ceiling. Ask classmates to list words that describe the mobile.

CURRICULUM
•CONNECTION•

Writing for Science

In science you need to observe carefully. You need to describe what you see, hear, feel, taste, and smell. Writing will help you do it. Writing will help you learn about the world of science.

Writing to Learn

Think and Observe ♦ Do you think any animals live in the desert? What do you see in the picture? If you were in the desert, what would it be like? Make an observation chart.

Write ♦ Write what you might see, hear, smell, and feel in the desert.

Writing in Your Journal

You have to read about what people do in all kinds of weather. Write about how you feel or what you do to have fun on a sunny, snowy, or rainy day.

Observation Chart

BOOKS TO ENJOY

 ## Read More About It

Gilberto and the Wind
by Marie Hall Ets
Discover how much the wind can do. Read about how a little boy enjoys the wind as his playmate.

Spring Book Festival Honor Book

The Cloud Book
by Tomie de Paola
Learn all about different kinds of clouds. Then you can tell what the weather will be.

 ## Book Report Idea   Paper Shape

Choose a book you like about weather or nature. Draw the outline of something in the book. Maybe it will be an animal, a tree, or the sun. Cut out the shape. Write your report on it. Hang the shape from a string and watch it move in the breeze.

Dawn
by
Uri Shulevitz
This book tells what happens every morning.

Adverbs

A. Write the adverb from each sentence. Then write if it tells **when** or **where**.

1. We fly kites here.

2. School starts early.

3. Rain was everywhere.

4. Today it is hot.

5. Jack went inside.

6. Soon Sue will leave.

7. What fell down?

8. Let's go now.

B. Write the sentences. Circle the adverbs that tell **how**.

9. Dale sang loudly again.

10. Ron quickly ran home.

11. He moved carefully.

12. Jan stood quietly.

13. They ate slowly.

14. Speak softly, please.

Opposites

C. Match the opposites.

15. shut   **a.** dry
16. on   **b.** open
17. wet   **c.** off

18. day   **d.** old
19. young   **e.** stand
20. sit   **f.** night

Paragraphs

D. Read the paragraph. Then follow
the directions.

Spring has arrived. White and
yellow flowers are popping up. Birds
are chirping. I love the cold snow.

21. Write the paragraph. Leave out the sentence
that does not belong.

22. Put a line under the sentence that tells the main idea.

23. Circle a sentence that gives a detail about
the main idea.

24. Write the sentence that does not keep to
the topic.

E. Pretend you are at the circus. Think about how
things look and sound. Follow these directions.

25. Write a sentence that tells how something looks.

26. Write a sentence that tells how something sounds.

USING LANGUAGE
TO
RESEARCH

=== **PART ONE** ===

Unit Theme   *People at Work*

Language Awareness   Sentences

=== **PART TWO** ===

Literature   "Junkyard Dinosaurs" by Sallie Luther

A Reason for Writing   Researching

Writing
IN YOUR JOURNAL

WRITER'S WARM-UP ◆ People do many jobs. Some people work in schools. Some work outside. Some workers help other people. What job do you know about? What kind of work would you like to do some day? Write about it in your journal.

Commands and Exclamations

Watch those firefighters.
What a hard job they have!

Watch those firefighters. is a command.
It tells someone to do something.
What a hard job they have! is an
exclamation. It shows strong feeling.

> ◆ A **command** gives an order.
>   It ends with a period ⊡.
>
> ◆ An **exclamation** shows strong feeling.
>   It ends with an exclamation mark ⏍.

◆ Copy the sentences.
Put one line under each command.
Put two lines under each exclamation.

1. Don't go across the street.

2. Stand on the sidewalk.

3. How wonderful that they are safe!

4. Give them room to work.

5. Don't get in their way.

6. What a long hose they brought!

7. How tired they look!

♦ Write the commands and exclamations.
Use capital letters and end marks correctly.

8. let us help you
9. what a day we had
10. how hot that fire felt
11. sit down over there
12. rest for a few minutes
13. how lucky we all were
14. get this bandage ready

15. put it on right here
16. how thirsty I am
17. drink some of this
18. how brave you were
19. what a good job they did
20. tell us all about it

Apply Write two commands and two exclamations.
Use some of these words in your sentences.

push   excited   pull   helpful   give   funny

2 Writing Four Kinds of Sentences

Statement	Many people help us each day.
Question	Where is Fulton School?
Command	Look both ways before you cross.
Exclamation	What a lot of milk you brought!

◆ Write the sentences below.
Begin each sentence with a capital letter.
Use the correct end mark.
Then write **S**, **Q**, **C**, or **E** to show
what kind of sentence each one is.

1. our friend works hard
2. will it be finished soon
3. watch out for the step
4. what a good job he did
5. did you bring some mail

6. walk between the lines
7. may we cross now
8. unload the crates here
9. that milk is for lunch
10. how good it will taste

◆ Write five sentences about the picture below.

11. Write a statement about the van.

12. Write a question about the tow truck.

13. Write a command that the police officer might say.

14. Write an exclamation about the traffic.

15. Write one more sentence about the picture. Then write **S, Q, C,** or **E** for your sentence.

◆ Now check your five sentences. Did you remember to use capital letters and correct end marks?

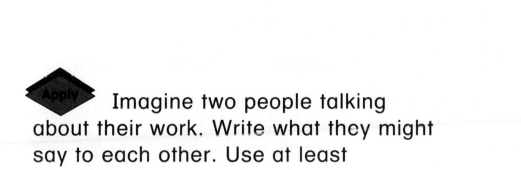

Apply Imagine two people talking about their work. Write what they might say to each other. Use at least two different kinds of sentences.

Changing Meaning with Word Order

The box is in the bag.   The bag is in the box.

Remember that words in a sentence must be in an order that makes sense. The meaning changes if the word order changes. Look at the words **bag** and **box** in the sentences above. The sentences have very different meanings.

◆ Change the order of the words in dark type. Write a sentence with a different meaning.

1. **Mr. Stein** helped **Ms. Santos**.

2. The **clock** is under the **sign**.

3. The **girl** looked at the **dog**.

4. **Her hand** is in **that bag**.

5. **His shoes** are larger than **my shoes**.

6. **That line** is shorter than **this line**.

7. **Ms. Santos** gave some money to **Mr. Stein**.

8. **My belt** is over **my sweater**.

Word order can change meaning.
The same words are in both sentences below.
One is a question. The other is
a statement that answers the question.

Is the bread ready now?
The bread is ready now.

◆ Change the word order of each question.
Use the same words to write a statement
that answers the question.

9. Does it smell good?

10. Can Marty try some?

11. Is it still hot?

12. Should we sit over there?

13. May I pay this bill?

14. Are Liz and Al hungry?

15. Will they meet us here?

◆**Apply** Pretend you are in a restaurant.
Write a question and a statement about it.
Use the same words in both sentences.

Clues to Word Meaning

Read this sentence.

> Mrs. Bailey's office is in a **skyscraper**, or very tall building.

The word **skyscraper** means "very tall building." You may not know the meaning of a new word when you read. Look at the other words in the sentence to get clues.

> ◆ A **context clue** helps you understand the meaning of a new word.

◆ Read each sentence and look for context clues. Then write what you think each word in dark type means.

1. She must **organize**, or sort out, all the papers on her desk.

   The word organize means ___.

2. Mrs. Bailey finishes her work **rapidly**, or quickly.

   The word **rapidly** means ___.

3. Now everything is neat and **tidy**!

   The word **tidy** means ___.

Write what you think each word in dark type means.

4. Moving quickly, Mrs. Bailey **scurries** to meet her family.

5. She wants to be **prompt**, or on time.

6. Mrs. Bailey **beams**, or smiles, when she sees her family.

7. Melissa is **overjoyed**, to see Mom, and Dad is happy, too.

8. They will **attempt**, or try, to buy a birthday present for Aunt Carol.

9. Sometimes it is hard to **locate**, or find, a gift.

10. They **select**, or choose, a cotton scarf.

11. They need to **purchase** one more thing. They need to buy a birthday card.

Apply Write a word that is new to you. Find it in this book or in another book. Look for context clues. Then write what you think your new word means.

How to Combine Sentences

Sometimes two sentences have ideas that go together. You can use a comma and the word **and** to combine them.

> **A. Maria loves planes.**
> **B. She wants to be a pilot.**
> **A + B. Maria loves planes, and she wants to be a pilot.**

Sentences **A** and **B** tell two ideas about Maria that go together. The two ideas are combined in sentences **A + B**.

You can combine other kinds of sentences, too. What kinds of sentences are combined below?

> **C. Open the door.**
> **D. Shut the window.**
> **C + D. Open the door, and shut the window.**

◆ Tell how to combine these sentences.

1. I heard sirens. A fire truck raced by.
2. Who baked bread? May I eat some?

Working Together

Use a comma and **and** to combine sentences in your group.

◆ Which sentences go together? Combine one sentence from each box. Write three new sentences.

The cars stopped.	Everyone sang along.
The band played.	I put them in a vase.
I picked flowers.	We crossed the street.

◆ Play guess-my-job! Each group member should combine one sentence pair below. Write your new sentence. Take turns acting out your jobs.

1. I drive. My riders go to school.

2. I have a tractor. I grow corn.

3. I run with my team. I kick the ball.

4. I read stories. I help you find books.

detail from mural "America Today" by Thomas Hart Benton, 1930
Courtesy of the Equitable Life Assurance Society of the United States.

USING LANGUAGE
TO
RESEARCH

=== **PART TWO** ===

Literature "Junkyard Dinosaurs" by Sallie Luther
A Reason for Writing Researching

CREATIVE
Writing

FINE ARTS ◆ Thomas Hart Benton painted this picture. He called the painting "Changing West." Look at the picture. What do you see? Give the painting a new title. What will you call it?

A Strategy for Researching

A Question Wheel

When you wonder about something, what do you do? Usually, you ask questions. Asking questions is a good way to learn things.

◆ Look at this picture of a dinosaur. What do you wonder about it? Read the question. Can you think of other questions to ask? Tell your questions.

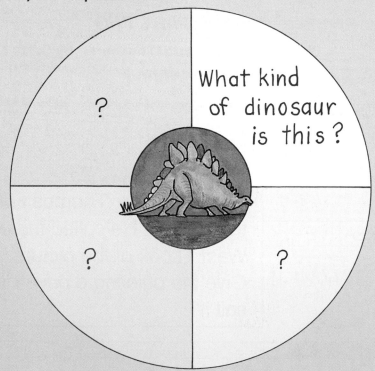

What kind of dinosaur is this? It is a stegosaurus. Do you know answers to your other questions? How can you find out?

Next you will read "Junkyard Dinosaurs."
A picture from this article is inside the
question wheel. Do you wonder about it? What
questions could you ask about it?

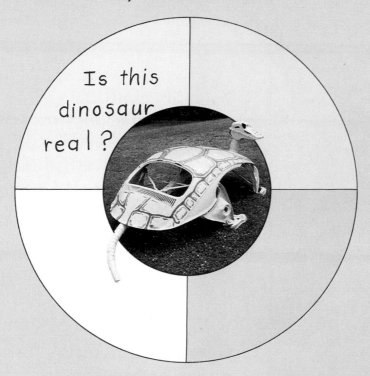

Is this dinosaur real?

 Work with a partner. Think of more
questions about the picture. Then read
"Junkyard Dinosaurs." See if you find
answers to some of your questions.

Apply

♦ Tell how you thought of one question you
  asked.

♦ What question have you asked this week?
  What did you find out?

JUNKYARD DINOSAURS

By Sallie Luther

When Jim Gary goes on a dinosaur hunt, he doesn't pack a pick and shovel. Instead, he loads up his blow torch and tool kit. Jim isn't a scientist searching for fossils. He's a sculptor with a rare specialty. Jim Gary designs dinosaurs— like this *Tyrannosaurus*— from junk!

As a teenager, Jim was crazy about cars. He'd comb auto junkyards looking for parts to rebuild his old cars. It didn't take Jim long to see that some of those auto parts looked a lot like animal parts. Soon he could imagine skulls and ribs and backbones among the crankcases and carburetors. Now, Jim has combined his love of cars, his interest in dinosaurs, and his talent as a sculptor into a career.

How does Jim make his "Twentieth Century Dinosaurs"? First he pokes around until he finds a part he wants. Then he cuts or unbolts it from the jumble of junked cars. Next, the part must be cleaned and cut to the size and shape Jim needs. Finally it must be welded to other parts and painted.

This isn't quick work. Sometimes it takes him months or even years to build one of his beasts. Jim's big *Apatosaurus* has been his largest work so far.

It's made from over 500 auto parts. Each was "dug up" in New Jersey junkyards.

Most of the parts that Jim uses come from cars that are over ten years old. He says the older parts have more "character" than the ones from newer makes of automobiles.

The orange and yellow dinosaurs on page 295 are good examples of what Jim means. The bodies of these two beasts used to be the roofs of old Volkswagens!

Last year Jim's work was on display at the Carnegie Museum of Natural History in Pittsburgh. Now it's at Jim's studio in Red Bank, New Jersey.

Jim's exhibit is always very popular. But it's not meant to be all fun. Jim wants to show the importance of *recycling,* or using things more than once. He uses things that people throw away to make his amazing sculptures.

LITERATURE: Nonfiction

This is Jim Gary's way to say that we all should be less wasteful. If not, we may one day find ourselves as extinct as the dinosaurs.

Library Link ◆ *If you liked this article from Ranger Rick, look for other interesting articles in this magazine.*

Reader's Response

Would you like to watch Jim Gary work? Tell why or why not.

JUNKYARD DINOSAURS

 ## Responding to Literature

1. What can you recycle? Collect things like food containers, boxes, and other "junk." Use them to make a real or make-believe animal.

2. What things are recycled in your town? Find out, and make a class list.

3. Jim Gary's hobby was rebuilding old cars. What hobbies do you and your friends have?

 ## Writing to Learn

Think and Wonder ◆ Did you ever wonder what happens to garbage after it is put in a truck? Draw a garbage truck in the middle of a question wheel. Think of four questions you could ask the people who collect your garbage.

Question Wheel

Write ◆ Write your questions in your wheel.

When you pick up a new book, how can you know what is in it? Look at these pages from the beginning of two books.

The **title** is the name of the book.
The **author** is the person who wrote the book.

◆ What have you learned from these pages? Write your answers to these questions.

1. What is the title of the book about locks?

2. Who wrote the book about safes?

3. Who is the author of <u>How a Lock Is Made</u>?

4. What is the title of Julie Thorp's book?

You can learn more about a book from its **table of contents**. It lists what is in the book. It also tells you on what page each part of the book begins.

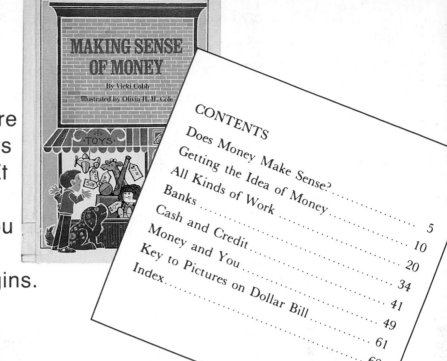

◆ Read this table of contents. What can you learn from it? Write your answers.

5. What is the name of the first part of the book?

6. On what page does the part about **Banks** begin?

7. What part begins on page 49?

8. Suppose you want to learn about pictures on a dollar bill. What page will you turn to?

Apply Talk with a partner about using a table of contents. Discuss how it can help you choose the right book. Make up a skit about your ideas.

Writing a Book Report

One way to share a book you have read is to write a book report. It will let your classmates know about a book they might like to read. Follow these steps for a good book report.

- ◆ Write the title and underline it. The first, last, and all important words begin with capital letters.
- ◆ Write the name of the author.
- ◆ Tell the main idea of the book. Give the name of the most important character.
- ◆ Tell one or two things that happen in the book. Do not give away the ending.
- ◆ Give your opinion of the book. If you like it, tell why.

Read Todd's book report.
Does it make you want to read this book?

Todd Rillo

Title: Nate the Great
Author: Marjorie Weinman Sharmat
    This book is about a boy named Nate.
He is a detective and likes to solve
mysteries. When he does, he wears a special
hat and coat. I think this book is funny.
Read it to find out how to be a detective.

Share a book that you like.
Write a book report about it on a form like this one.
Remember to underline the title.

Title ___

Author ___

   This book is about ___.

In my opinion, this book is ___.

Apply Take turns sharing your book reports.
Which books do you think you would like to read?
Write the titles to remind you about the books.

Sharing a Book

How can you tell your classmates about a book you really like? Writing a book report is one way. Here are some other ways.

Hang It on the Line

Cut out a paper sock. Write the title and author of your book on it. Write some story details, or draw a picture from the story. Hang it up on the line.

Build It in a Box

Build a scene in a small box. Use paper, clay, small toys, or other props. Write the title and author of your book on a sign. Display the boxes in your room.

Fly a Book Kite

Cut out a paper kite. Write the title and author of your book. Draw a picture for the beginning and the middle of the book. Write some interesting words from your book on a long paper tail. Hang the kite in your classroom.

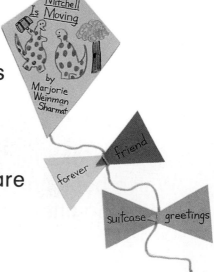

Apply   Think of an interesting way to share a book. Give reasons why you think your classmates will enjoy your book, too.

Using the Library

Your own **library card** is like a special passport. It allows you to borrow hundreds of books from your **library**, a few at a time.

You will find **fiction** and **nonfiction** books. Fiction books are about people, places, and things that are made up by the author. Nonfiction books have information about real people, places, and things.

What else does your library have? Today many libraries have **magazines**, **audio and video tapes**, **records**, **films**, and **computers**. Often there are special collections in a **display case**.

What have you learned about a library? Write your answers to these questions.

1. Besides books, a library may have ___.
2. ___ books are about made-up things.
3. You can find facts in ___ books.
4. You might see dinosaur models in a ___.

Apply   Find a fiction and a nonfiction library book about the same subject. For example, you might choose <u>Danny and the Dinosaur</u> by Syd Hoff and <u>Dinosaur Time</u> by Peggy Parish.

You know how to find information in books. Did you know that you can get information from people, too? When you **interview** someone, you ask questions and the person gives you answers.

Plan the questions you want to ask. Then listen carefully to the answers. Write some words to help you remember the answers.

Lisa used the **5 W's** to interview Dr. Francisco Caras. She asked questions about **who**, **what**, **when**, **where**, and **why**. She wrote some of his answers.

What is your job?   dinosaur expert

Where do you work?   The Natural History Museum

When did you first get   When he was six
interested in   —read about them
dinasaurs?   —drew them
                                                   —built models

Who works with you?   two helpers

Why are dinosaurs   Dinosaurs make people use
so popular?   their imagination. They
                                               mix science and fantasy.

◆ Which person who works in your school would you like to know more about? Plan an interview with him or her. Write the answers on a form like the one below. The **5 W's** can help you get started. You may also think of other questions you want to ask.

Who will I interview? ___

What is your job? ___

Where do you work? ___

When do you work? ___

Who works with you? ___

Why do you like your job? ___

Apply ▸ Pretend you will interview Jim Gary, the sculptor of "Junkyard Dinosaurs." What questions would you want to ask him? What answers might you get? Act out this interview with a partner.

Writing a Report

In "Junkyard Dinosaurs" you learned a new use for junk. Jim Gary turns junk into art. What do your classmates think about using junk? You could take a poll to find out.

When you take a poll, you interview many people. You ask them all the same question or questions. You find out what they think.

Now you will take a poll. Later you will share what you learned with your classmates.

1 Prewriting

First you need to choose a topic. Then you need to take a poll about your topic.

Choose Your Topic ◆ With your class, think of questions to ask. Find some that can be answered Yes or No. For example: *Should we find new uses for junk?*

Form a small group. Let every child choose a different question. You will ask your question to members of your group.

Should we find new uses for junk?
Should we have homework every day?
Is it all right to trade lunches?
Do you like to read books?

Choose Your Plan ◆ These plans can help you take your poll.

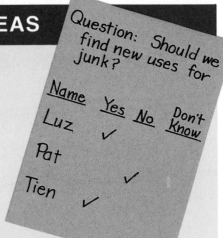

PREWRITING IDEAS

Plan One ◆ A Poll Chart

Make a poll chart. Write your topic question at the top. Write the names of children in your group. Then put a check mark to show each child's answer.

When you are finished, add up the Yes answers. Then add up the No and Don't Know answers. Now you have three good facts for your writing.

Plan Two ◆ A Question Wheel

You can ask more than one question if you like. Make a question wheel. Write your topic question in the middle. Then think of other questions about your topic. Write them around the outside.

Record answers to your topic question on a poll chart. Write other interesting answers on the back.

2 Writing

Now write about your poll. You may begin with your topic question. Then tell what answers you got. Tell about the Yes, No, and Don't Know answers.

Did some children give reasons for their answers? Did you ask additional questions? Add some of this information. It will make your report interesting.

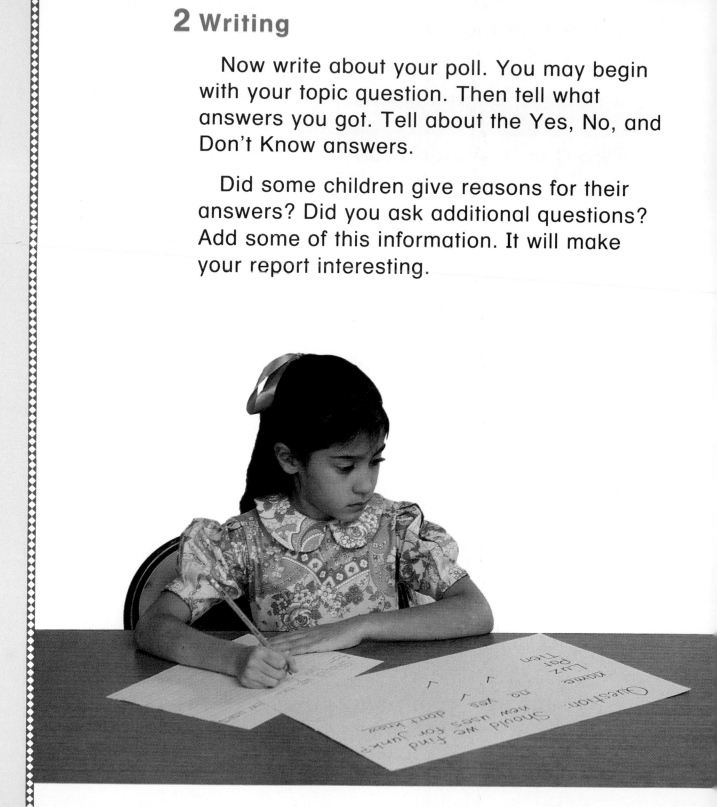

3 Revising

Look at how Rosa revised her report. She changed some words. She added a reason.

REVISING
MARKS

— cross out

∧ add

Should we find new uses for junk? Pat said no.

Junk can be ∧ danjerus.
  (dirty and) inserted above

Luz and tien said yes.

Luz said some old stuff
  (things) written above crossed-out *stuff*

is still useful. ∧
  (are) written above crossed-out *is*; *Tien said cans can be recycled.* added

REVISING IDEA

Read your report to yourself, then to a partner. Ask if your information is clear.

◆ Should I add any information?

◆ Can I make my report clearer?

Grammar Check ◆ Did I use different types of sentences?

Now revise your report to make it better.

4 Proofreading

Find any mistakes you need to fix. These questions can help.

♦ Did I indent the first word?

♦ Did I spell each word correctly?

♦ Did I use capital letters correctly?

♦ Did I use the correct mark at the end of each sentence?

Now add a title. Make a neat copy of your report.

PROOFREADING MARKS	
¶	indent
⬭	check spelling
≡	capital letter

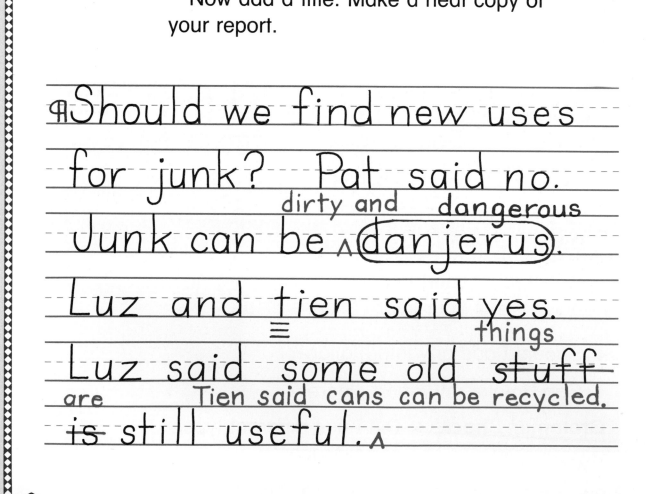

¶Should we find new uses for junk? Pat said no.
dirty and   dangerous
Junk can be ∧(danjerus).
Luz and tien said yes.
≡
                    things
Luz said some old stuff
are   Tien said cans can be recycled.
is still useful.∧

5 Publishing

Here are two ways you might share your report.

PUBLISHING IDEAS

Share Aloud

Give a talk. Start by writing your question on the chalkboard. Then tell how your group answered it. Ask the rest of the class to answer it, too. Let them raise hands to answer Yes or No. Ask volunteers to give their reasons.

Share in Writing

Post all the reports on a bulletin board. Beside each report put cards that say Yes and No. Read the reports. Answer each report's question. Put your name on the Yes or No card.

> My Report
> Should we find new uses for junk? Pat said no. Junk can be dirty and dangerous. Luz and Tien said yes. Luz said some old things are still useful. Tien said cans can be recycled.

yes
Katie
Jennifer
Robert

no
Pablo
Lisa

CURRICULUM ·CONNECTION·

 ## Writing for Social Studies

When you ask questions and search for answers, you are doing research. Asking and answering questions is important in social studies. It is a good way to learn. You will use writing as you ask and answer questions.

Carl

Dave

Writing to Learn

Think and Wonder ◆ Choose one worker from the pictures. What do you wonder about this person? What do you wonder about the worker's job? Make a question wheel.

Write ◆ Write the worker's name in the center of your wheel. Write your questions around it.

Question Wheel

 ## Writing in Your Journal

What kind of work did you find out about in this unit? Did you learn about new jobs? Write about one job you would like to know more about.

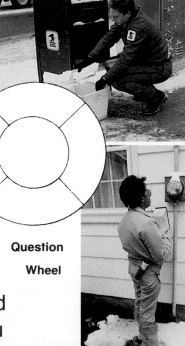

Maria

BOOKS TO ENJOY

Read More About It

Martin's Hats *by Joan W. Blos*
All through the day Martin is very busy. He imagines he is doing many kinds of work. Look for the special hat he wears for each different job.

I Can Be a Pilot
by June Behrens
Read this book to find out all about flying an airplane.

Book Report Idea   News Show

Pretend you are a news reporter. You report on books for children. Plan an interesting report about a book you like. Practice saying it out loud. Then record it with a tape recorder. Your classmates can listen to your news report.

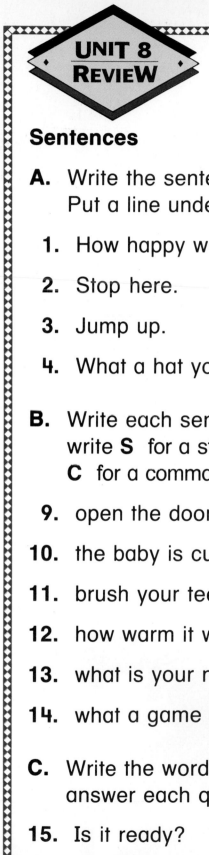

Sentences

A. Write the sentences. Circle each command.
Put a line under each exclamation.

1. How happy we are!

2. Stop here.

3. Jump up.

4. What a hat you have!

5. Move the box.

6. How pretty you look!

7. What a day it was!

8. Stand still.

B. Write each sentence correctly. Then
write **S** for a statement, **Q** for a question,
C for a command, or **E** for an exclamation.

9. open the door

10. the baby is cute

11. brush your teeth

12. how warm it was

13. what is your name

14. what a game it is

C. Write the words in a different order to
answer each question.

15. Is it ready?

16. Can they go?

Finding Information

D. Write the answer for each clue.

nonfiction book	fiction book
library card	author
table of contents	title

17. It is the person who wrote the book.

18. It lists what is in the book.

19. It is about made-up people, places, and things.

20. It is the name of the book.

21. It is about real people, places, and things.

22. It allows you to borrow books.

E. Read the interview notes. Copy the report.
Write the missing parts.

What is your name?	Rose Gómez
What is your job?	postal worker
Where do you work?	post office
When do you work?	Tuesday to Saturday

Ms. ___ has a busy job. She is a ___

at the ___ . She works from ___ .

Sentences

A. Write the sentence in each pair.

    1. **a.** Opened the box
       b. Sue opened the box.

    2. **a.** Your blue hat
       b. Your new hat is blue.

B. Write each sentence. Circle the naming part.
    Put a line under the telling part.

    3. The train left late.   **5.** He visited us.

    4. They waited for it.   **6.** Our family went home.

C. Write the sentences. Circle each command.
    Put a line under each exclamation.

    7. What a heavy book that is!
    8. Pick up your clothes.
    9. Wait over here.
   10. How late you are!

D. Write each sentence correctly.

   11. play outside   **13.** where did you go

   12. the leaves blew   **14.** how lucky we are

Nouns

E. Write the nouns that mean more than one.

15. class classes   **17.** goose geese

16. socks sock   **18.** peach peaches

F. Write each name, title, or special day correctly.

19. ms gail daly

20. new year's day

21. crow boy

22. wednesday

Pronouns

G. Write the sentences. Use **She, It, They**, and **We** for the words in ( ).

23. (Peg and I) hiked.

24. (Rose and Meg) camped.

25. (Tara) met us.

26. (The tent) fell.

H. Write each sentence. Use **I** or **me** correctly.

27. Joy and (I, me) baked bread.

28. Lucy passed it to (I, me).

29. Rob saw Tory and (I, me).

30. Now (I, me) am ready.

Verbs

I. Write each sentence. Use the
correct verb in ( ).

   31. It (was, were) very cold in the mountains.

   32. Maria and Clara (is, are) in the camper.

   33. Herb (walk, walks) down a rocky path.

   34. Do you (have, has) a blanket?

   35. Last night Sondra (fix, fixed) the tent.

J. Write the verbs that tell about the past.

   36. went go
   37. does did
   38. ran run
   39. take took
   40. came come
   41. gave gives

Adjectives

K. Write the adjective in each sentence.
Then write **how many** or **what kind** for each one.

   42. Pam found some balloons.

   43. Giraffes have long necks.

   44. Tom watched three beavers.

   45. Karen and Cora collect pink shells.

L. Add **-er** or **-est** to the adjective in ( ).
Write each sentence. Use the new adjective.

    46. My hair is (short) than your hair.

    47. Don's hair is the (short) of all.

    48. Today is (cool) than yesterday.

    49. Saturday was the (cool) day this week.

M. Write each sentence. Use **a** or **an**.

    50. She fed (a, an) elephant.

    51. Mike saw (a, an) snake.

    52. Barbara rode (a, an) horse.

    53. Is that (a, an) alligator?

Adverbs

N. Write the adverb from each sentence.
Then write **when, where,** or **how** for each one.

    54. We will leave soon.

    55. Dr. Lane clapped softly.

    56. Cross the street carefully.

    57. Ellen walked there on Sunday.

    58. She will return tomorrow.

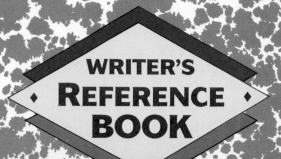

WRITER'S
REFERENCE
BOOK

Word Finder

Main Entry Words

animal 324	cook 327	happy 329	put 332
		hot 330	
bad 324	fruit 327		sad 332
big 325			say 333
break 325	get 328	little 330	
building 326	go 328	look 331	
	good 329		vegetable 333
cold 326	ground 329	make 331	well 334

Synonyms for Main Entry Words

apartment house 326	earth 329	lay 332	school 326
apple 327	easily 334	lettuce 333	see 331
awful 324	elephant 324	library 326	set 332
	excellent 329	lion 324	shape 331
	expertly 334	lonely 332	short 330
bake 327	explode 325	loud 325	shout 333
banana 327			sick 324
boil 327	fish 324	miserable 332	smash 325
build 331	floor 329		sorry 332
burning 330	fly 328		spicy 330
buy 328	frosty 326	onion 333	stare 331
	fry 327	orange 327	
call 333	giraffe 324	peach 327	tear 325
carefully 334	glad 329	peek 331	tiny 330
carrot 333	grill 327	place 332	
catch 328		pleasant 329	
cheerful 329	house 326	potato 333	walk 328
cool 326	huge 325		warm 330
crack 325		quiet 330	watch 331
create 331	icy 326		whisper 333
	important 325	recite 333	win 328
dangerous 324		ride 328	
dirt 329	jolly 329	right 329	
dog 324	jump 328	run 328	young 330

animal ♦ a living creature.
A crocodile is a long <u>animal</u>.

dog a pet that barks and that has four legs and a tail.
My <u>dog</u> can sit up and shake hands.

elephant a large animal with a long trunk, floppy ears, tusks, and four legs.
I fed peanuts to that <u>elephant</u>.

fish an animal that has fins, gills, and a tail, and that lives in water.
A <u>fish</u> lives in fresh or salt water.

giraffe a very tall animal that has four long legs and a long neck.
The <u>giraffe</u> can peek over the fence.

lion a large, powerful member of the cat family.
The <u>lion</u> hunts for its food.

bad ♦ not good.
I have a <u>bad</u> cold.

awful very bad or unpleasant.
The burnt food smelled <u>awful</u>.

dangerous not safe.
We won't drive on a <u>dangerous</u> road.

sick in bad health.
When I feel <u>sick</u>, I go to bed.

big ◆ large in size.
The <u>big</u> plane flew away.

huge   unusually large.
The <u>huge</u> cloud blocked the sun.

important   of much value.
The mayor has an <u>important</u> job.

loud   easy to hear.
The drums made a <u>loud</u> sound.

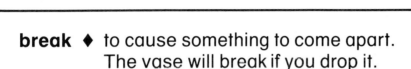

break ◆ to cause something to come apart.
The vase will <u>break</u> if you drop it.

crack   to damage something without having
it fall apart.
Ice can <u>crack</u> when you walk on it
if it is not thick.

explode   to blow apart.
The balloon will <u>explode</u> if you
blow too much air into it.

smash   to break into many small pieces.
A glass will <u>smash</u> if you drop it.

tear   to rip something apart.
Did you <u>tear</u> the paper into two
pieces?

building ♦ something having walls, floors, and a roof, where people live or work. That <u>building</u> has large windows.

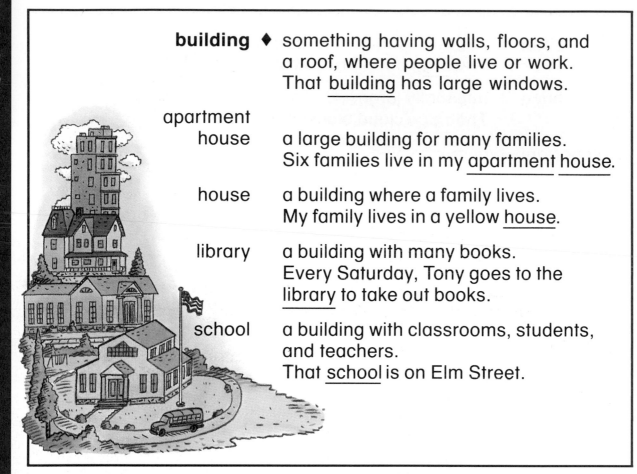

apartment house   a large building for many families. Six families live in my <u>apartment</u> <u>house</u>.

house   a building where a family lives. My family lives in a yellow <u>house</u>.

library   a building with many books. Every Saturday, Tony goes to the <u>library</u> to take out books.

school   a building with classrooms, students, and teachers. That <u>school</u> is on Elm Street.

cold ♦ having a very low temperature. When the weather gets <u>cold</u>, I sneeze.

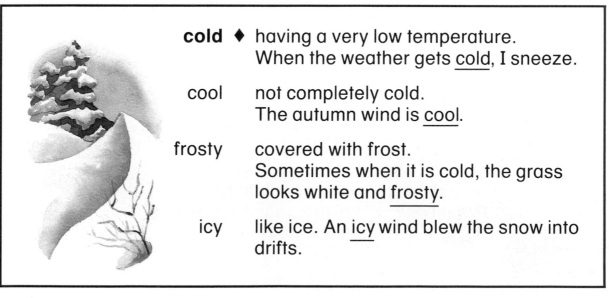

cool   not completely cold. The autumn wind is <u>cool</u>.

frosty   covered with frost. Sometimes when it is cold, the grass looks white and <u>frosty</u>.

icy   like ice. An <u>icy</u> wind blew the snow into drifts.

cook ◆ to prepare food with heat.
We <u>cook</u> our dinner every night.

bake   to cook in an oven.
The house smells wonderful
when we <u>bake</u> bread.

boil   to cook in water.
We <u>boil</u> beets in a pot.

fry   to cook in fat or oil.
Let's <u>fry</u> the fish.

grill   to cook over an open fire.
We <u>grill</u> hamburgers in the summer.

fruit ◆ the part of the plant that has seeds
and may usually be eaten.
I love to eat <u>fruit</u> in the summer.

apple   a round red, green, or yellow fruit
that grows on trees.
This <u>apple</u> is sweet and juicy.

banana   a long, curved fruit with thick,
yellow skin.
It is fun to peel a <u>banana</u>.

orange   a round fruit with a thick skin.
The juice is from this <u>orange</u>.

peach   a sweet, round fruit with fuzzy skin.
This juicy <u>peach</u> tastes so good!

get ♦ to own or have something.
John will <u>get</u> a dog for his birthday.

buy   to own after paying for something.
I earned money to <u>buy</u> this book.

catch   to capture something by trapping.
I can <u>catch</u> a ball with my mitt.

win   to get something in a contest.
Only one person can <u>win</u> the prize.

go ♦ to move to or from something.
We <u>go</u> to the store.

fly   to move in the air, using wings.
I saw a jet <u>fly</u> in the sky.

jump   to leap up or leap over something.
The horses <u>jump</u> over the fence.

ride   to move in or on something.
We <u>ride</u> in a train to the city.

run   to go faster than walking.
We can <u>run</u> until our legs hurt.

walk   to move one foot in front of the other.
When I <u>walk</u>, I look at everything.

good ◆ pleasing, right or proper.
Dan is a good boy to help his brother.

excellent   very, very good. Jan practices every day and is an excellent juggler.

pleasant   nice or enjoyable.
We had a pleasant time at the zoo.

right   correct or proper.
It is right to tell the truth.

ground ◆ the surface of the earth.
We planted flowers in the ground.

dirt   the loose, top layer of the ground.
The wind blew dirt into our house.

earth   soil or ground.
Fill the flowerpot with earth.

floor   the part of a room we walk on.
There is a red rug on the floor.

happy ◆ feeling well and pleased.
I am happy when I visit Grandma.

cheerful   full of good feeling.
Jo is always smiling and cheerful.

glad   happy about something.
Mary is glad you came to visit her.

jolly   very, very happy.
Tom is so jolly he laughs all the time.

hot ◆ having a very high temperature.
The sun makes the sand <u>hot</u>.

burning   hot enough to cause pain.
Anne's <u>burning</u> skin feels painful.

spicy   having a hot or peppery taste.
This is a <u>spicy</u> sauce.

warm   not quite hot.
The spring air feels <u>warm</u>.

little ◆ not of great size.
Tom's balloon was <u>little</u>.

quiet   hard to hear.
Kevin sang in a <u>quiet</u> voice.

short   not very tall.
I am too <u>short</u> to reach the shelf.

tiny   very, very small.
The <u>tiny</u> bug sat on my finger.

young   not many years old.
A <u>young</u> cat is a kitten.

look ◆ to see something with your eyes.
Look at the shooting star!

peek to look at something secretly.
I can peek at the chipmunk from here.

see to be able to look at something.
Cindy can see the bus coming.

stare to keep looking at something
for a long time, without blinking.
We stare at the fish and
the fish stare at us.

watch to observe something for a while.
I like to watch the birds fly south.

make ◆ to cause something to be or to happen.
Rosa can make lunch for herself.

build to construct something from
materials.
Let's build a wooden clubhouse.

create to think up something new.
Can you create a new game?

shape to give form to something.
Nancy can shape clay into a turtle.

put ♦ to move something to a place.
Bill <u>put</u> his bike in the garage.

lay   to put something down.
<u>Lay</u> the mat in front of the door.

place   to move something to a certain spot.
<u>Place</u> this dish on top of the others.

set   to arrange something somewhere
for a reason.
He <u>set</u> seedlings out in the garden.

sad ♦ unhappy.
I was <u>sad</u> when my dog ran away.

lonely   alone and sad.
Kathy felt <u>lonely</u> when her best friend
moved away.

miserable   very, very unhappy.
Josh was <u>miserable</u> until his sick
puppy got better.

sorry   sad about something that
was said or done.
I was <u>sorry</u> I broke the plate.

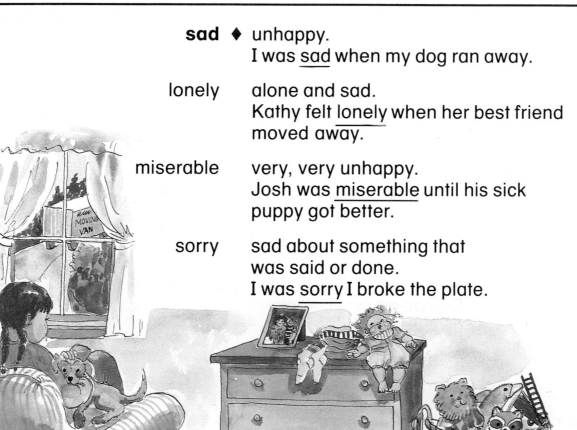

say ♦ to put into words.
I always <u>say</u> what I think.

call to speak aloud.
Will you <u>call</u> my name next?

recite to speak from memory.
We <u>recite</u> the Pledge of
Allegiance every day.

shout to say in a loud voice.
Conductors <u>shout</u>, "All aboard!"

whisper to say in a very quiet voice.
How softly can you <u>whisper</u> the clue?

vegetable ♦ a plant whose roots, leaves,
stems, or flowers can be eaten.
Celery is a green <u>vegetable</u>.

carrot a long, thin, orange root.
I like to eat a raw <u>carrot</u>.

lettuce a plant with crisp, green leaves.
Scot puts <u>lettuce</u> in his salad.

onion a bulb of the lily family.
Do you cry when you cut
an <u>onion</u>?

potato a hard vegetable with a thin
skin that grows underground.
A <u>potato</u> can be baked, boiled,
fried, or mashed.

well ♦ in a good way.
The party is going <u>well</u>.

carefully   with care.
Mr. Gomez climbed down <u>carefully</u>.

easily   without trouble.
We <u>easily</u> followed the map.

expertly   very, very well.
You played that song <u>expertly</u>.

A Guide to Spelling

Here are five helpful spelling rules. Knowing them will help you spell many words. Remember to use these rules when you write.

1. If a word ends in **e**,

    ♦ drop the **e** when you add a suffix that begins with a vowel.

    ride + ing = riding

    ♦ keep the **e** when you add a suffix that begins with a consonant.

    love + ly = lovely

2. Many words end in one vowel and one consonant. Double that consonant when you add a suffix that begins with a vowel.

    cut + ing = cutting

3. If a word ends in a vowel and **y**, keep the **y** when you add a suffix.

    say + ing = saying

4. If a word ends in a consonant and **y**,

    ♦ keep the **y** when you add **-ing**.

    fly + ing = flying

    ♦ change the **y** to **i** when you add other suffixes.

    fly + es = flies   **happy + ly = happily**

5. When you choose between **ie** and **ei**,

♦ usually use **ie**.

lie   **field**

♦ use **ei** after **c** or for the long **a** sound.

receive   **neighbor**

Words Often Misspelled

1. again
2. always
3. among
4. answer
5. anything
6. been
7. break
8. busy
9. children
10. color
11. coming
12. cough
13. could
14. doctor
15. done
16. early
17. easy
18. every
19. forty
20. guess
21. hear
22. heard
23. here
24. knew
25. know
26. laid
27. many
28. much
29. often
30. pretty
31. raise
32. said
33. shoes
34. since
35. some
36. sometime
37. sugar
38. sure
39. their
40. there
41. they
42. threw
43. through
44. tired
45. together
46. too
47. two
48. very
49. where
50. writing

Your Spelling Notebook

Another way to help your spelling is to keep a notebook of special words. Look for words in the books you read. Find words that you think are hard to spell. Write these words in your spelling notebook. When you need to use a word, you can look it up.

Make a notebook page for each letter of the alphabet. Keep the pages in ABC order. This will make your special words easy to find when you need them.

Words Often Written

Below are words that many students, like you, have used when writing. When you proofread, you can use this list for help.

1. a	11. go	21. in	31. said	41. up
2. all	12. got	22. is	32. saw	42. was
3. and	13. had	23. it	33. she	43. we
4. are	14. have	24. like	34. so	44. went
5. at	15. he	25. me	35. that	45. were
6. be	16. her	26. my	36. the	46. when
7. but	17. him	27. of	37. then	47. why
8. day	18. his	28. on	38. there	48. with
9. for	19. home	29. one	39. they	49. would
10. get	20. I	30. out	40. to	50. you

Index

Acknowledgments continued from page ii.

Permissions: We wish to thank the following authors, publishers, agents, corporations, and individuals for their permission to reprint coyrighted materials. Page 22: Excerpt from *I Know a Lady* by Charlotte Zolotow, pictures by James Stevenson. Text copyright © 1984 by Charlotte Zolotow. Illustrations copyright © 1984 by James Stevenson. Reprinted by permission of Greenwillow Books (a division of William Morrow & Co., Inc.). Page 62: *A Bird Can Fly* by Douglas Florian. Copyright © 1980 by Douglas Florian. Reprinted by permission of Greenwillow Books (a division of William Morrow & Co., Inc.). Page 100: *The Paper Crane* by Molly Bang. Copyright © 1985 by Molly Garrett Bang. Reprinted by permission of Greenwillow Books (a division of William Morrow & Co., Inc.). Page 142: "I am Running in a Circle" from *The New Kid on the Block* by Jack Prelutsky. Copyright © 1984 by Jack Prelutsky. Used by permission of Greenwillow Books (a division of William Morrow & Co., Inc.). Page 143: "Berries on the bushes…" from *Blackberry Ink* by Eve Merriam. Copyright © 1985 by Eve Merriam. All rights reserved. Reprinted by permission of Marian Reiner for the author. "Unusual Shoelaces" by X.J. Kennedy. Copyright © 1975 by X.J. Kennedy. Reprinted by permission of Curtis Brown, Ltd. Page 144: "I Left My Head" from *See My Lovely Poison Ivy* by Lilian Moore. Copyright © 1975 by Lilian Moore. Reprinted by permission of Marian Reiner for the author. "I woke up one morning…" from *A Rumbudgin of Nonsense* by Arnold Spilka. All rights reserved. Reprinted by permission of Marian Reiner for the author. Page 146: "Up you go, Down you see…" Reprinted by permission of Philomel Books from *Chinese Mother Goose Rhymes* selected and edited by Robert Wyndham, © 1968 by Robert Wyndham. Page 147: The poem "Dilly Dilly Piccalilli" from *Father Fox's Penny Rhymes* by Clyde Watson, (Thomas Y. Crowell) illustrated by Wendy Watson. Text copyright © 1971 by Clyde Watson. Illustrations copyright © 1971 by Wendy Watson. Reprinted by permission of Harper & Row, Publishers, Inc. Page 148: The poem "Rope Rhyme" from *Honey I Love*, by Eloise Greenfield (Thomas Y. Crowell) illustrated by Diane and Leo Dillon. Text copyright © 1987 by Eloise Greenfield. Reprinted by permission of Harper & Row, Publishers, Inc. Page 150: "Balloono" from *Early in the Morning* by Charles Causley. Published by Viking Kestrel. Reprinted by permission of David Higham Associates. Page 151: "Catching-Song" by Eleanor Farjeon. Reprinted by permssion of Harold Ober Associates. Page 182: Excerpts from *Stringbean's Trip to the Shining Sea* by Vera B. Williams and Jennifer Williams. Copyright © 1988 by Vera B. Williams and Jennifer Williams. Reprinted by permission of Greenwillow Books (a division of William Morrow & Co., Inc.). Page 218: "California Ho" from *The Josefina Story Quilt* by Eleanor Coerr, pictures by Bruce Degan. Text copyright © 1986 by Eleanor Coerr, illustrations copyright © 1986 by Bruce Degan. Reprinted by permission of Harper & Row, Publishers, Inc. Page 256: Illustrated excerpt from *Owl Moon* by Jane Yolen, illustrated by John Schoenherr, text © 1987 by Jane Yolen, illustrations © 1987 by John Schoenherr. Reprinted by permission of Philomel Books. Page 294: "Junkyard Dinosaurs" by Sallie Luther. Reprinted from the November 1983 issue of *Ranger Rick* magazine, with permission from the publisher, the National Wildlife Federation. Copyright 1983 NWF.

C D E F G H I J—VH—96 95 94 93 92 91 90